R S P B

THE

BIRDWATCHER'S

L O G B O O K

R S P B

THE

BIRDWATCHER'S

L O G B O O K

Willow Books
Collins
Grafton Street, London
1986

Willow Books
William Collins & Co Ltd
London Glasgow Sydney Auckland

British Library Cataloguing in Publication Data
1. Birds – Great Britain – Identification
I. Royal Society for the Protection of Birds
598.2941 QL690.G7

ISBN 0 00 218218 1

First published 1986
Copyright © Lennard Books 1986

Made by Lennard Books
Mackerye End, Harpenden
Herts AL5 5DR

Compiled by Sylvia Sullivan
Other contributors Frank Hamilton, Rob Hume, Michael Langman,
Roy Leverton, Steve Rooke, Tim Stowe, John Wilson
Editor Michael Leitch
Designed by David Pocknell's Company Ltd
Illustrations by Ian Lewington and Rob Hume
Production Reynolds Clark Associates Ltd
Printed and bound in Spain by
TONSA, San Sebastian

Contents

Bird Recognition

A Key to the Illustrations

Introduction

While the most obvious badge of a birdwatcher may be his binoculars, the fact that he always carries a notebook and pencil is a much more telling sign. Of course, you do not *need* to take notes to enjoy looking at birds, but if you do you will soon become a more expert and skilful birdwatcher.

Apart from the personal satisfaction of having something to look back on, one of the reasons birdwatchers are always encouraged to take notes is that they are constantly adding to the general pool of knowledge about birds and their environment. I am sure that one of the main reasons for the success of bird protection in this country is the enormous contribution made by amateurs. Even today there are still relatively few professional ornithologists and conservationists, and almost all of them started off as keen amateur birdwatchers.

My own interest began with the school natural history society and during those early days I made particular studies of the grey heron and sparrowhawk. It is ironic that these species were two of the major victims of the widespread use of organochlorine insecticides in the late 1950s and early '60s, and because of this I was to look closely at them again during the time I worked for the Nature Conservancy (as it was then). Thanks to the alarm raised by ordinary birdwatchers about the decline of the peregrine, sparrowhawk and other birds of prey, an investigation produced evidence that led to the withdrawal from general agricultural use of DDT, dieldrin and other persistent compounds. More recently, concern about lead poisoning in mute swans has encouraged fishermen to start using non-toxic weights. So never underestimate the value of your own observations and records.

Anyone who is enthusiastic about their hobby will want to keep some sort of record of their progress. Birdwatching offers endless scope: some people have boxes full of old field notebooks, others diligently transfer their records onto meticulously ordered card indexes, computers or into beautifully bound diaries. And that is the purpose of this book. It is not meant to be taken into the field, but to serve as a reminder of some of your best days' birdwatching and the exciting birds you have seen. It is a book to be written up on a cold, dark winter's evening, when you will turn back the pages and reminisce with a smile.

Few of us can aspire to the vivid writing of naturalists like W. H. Hudson and Richard Jefferies, and even fewer have that extraordinary talent for drawing and sketching that makes Sir Peter Scott's *Travel Diaries* so delightful, but this small volume, your own personal birdwatching history, can be equally special. With a little care, it will be a book to be treasured by you and your family, a memento of a hobby that gives a lifetime's pleasure.

Ian Prestt, Director-General
The Royal Society for the Protection of Birds

R S P B
THE
BIRDWATCHER'S
LOGBOOK

——— Name ———

——— Address ———

——— Telephone ———

Your Birdwatching History

How did you become interested in birds? When did you start birdwatching? Is it a childhood passion that predates memory or do you recall a special outing with a parent, a present from a relative or an encounter with a particular bird that sparked off your curiosity? Many of us remember with great affection an early friend or teacher who fostered that enthusiasm. Use this page to record your own birdwatching history. Delve back into your early notes and memories or, if you have recently taken up birdwatching, here is an excellent chance to start as you mean to go on!

RSPB MEMBERSHIP NO.		YEAR JOINED	
RSPB MEMBERS' GROUP		SECRETARY	
FIRST INTEREST IN BIRDS			

FIRST OUTING

100TH SPECIES	DATE	PLACE
200TH SPECIES	DATE	PLACE
300TH SPECIES	DATE	PLACE

OTHER MEMBERSHIPS

ORGANIZATION	YEAR JOINED
ORGANIZATION	YEAR JOINED
ORGANIZATION	YEAR JOINED
ORGANIZATION	YEAR JOINED

The Birdwatcher's Code

Of course, it's always other people, never ourselves, who are guilty of dropping litter or failing to shut a farm gate. And it is still amazing to see the numbers of people who, well aware that they are visiting a nature reserve, will pick armfuls of wild flowers instead of leaving them for other people to enjoy. Naturally, the Country Code applies to birdwatchers as much as to other users of the countryside, but for extra guidance the Birdwatcher's Code was devised by birdwatching and conservation organizations.

The Code has been frequently published, but we make no apology for reprinting it here. Every birdwatcher has a responsibility not only to the birds which give us so much pleasure, but to set an example to others. This is particularly true when birdwatching in groups. Where one or two birdwatchers may go unnoticed, large numbers are much more conspicuous and the damage they can cause in their enthusiasm is that much greater. It is a great shame when public opinion is alienated, especially with so innocent a pastime. Birdwatchers can be a large and powerful force on the side of nature conservation, so make sure you follow these ten simple guidelines.

1. The welfare of the bird must come first. Whatever your particular interest, if you keep this maxim uppermost in your mind, you will not go far wrong.
2. Habitat must be protected.
3. Keep disturbance to birds and their habitat to a minimum. Resist the temptation to inspect nests during the breeding season – you could be opening the way for predators. Similarly, if vegetation has to be moved for the purpose of photography, make sure plants and twigs are tied back (never cut) and are carefully replaced afterwards. Disturbance to feeding birds in winter can be reduced by good fieldcraft and will give you better views of the birds too.
4. If you find a rare bird think carefully about whom you should tell. If you discover a rare bird breeding and feel that protection is necessary, contact the RSPB, otherwise it is better to keep the information to yourself. Disturbance at or near the nest of species on Schedule I of the Wildlife and Countryside Act, 1981, is a criminal offence.
5. Do not harass rare migrants.
6. Abide by the Wildlife and Countryside Act at all times.
7. Respect the rights of landowners. Do not enter land without permission. Comply with permit schemes. If you are leading a group, give advance notice of the visit, even if permits are not required.
8. Respect the rights of other people in the countryside.
9. Make your records available to the local bird recorder.
10. Behave abroad as you would when birdwatching at home.

How To Take Field Notes

Birds are deceptive – that is part of their charm. Wood pigeons are notorious for masquerading as other species, and how many times do we look hopefully at the silhouette of a bird flying overhead and then realize sheepishly that it is a carrion crow? Beware too the mimics of the bird world – can you tell the difference between the call of a green woodpecker and a starling imitating a green woodpecker?

The identification of birds is the first task of all birdwatchers. If you don't know what you're looking at, how can you study it? Field notes are an essential part of bird identification, so don't delay; take your field notes seriously from the beginning.

Getting close enough to watch birds properly is an art in itself and we wonder how many of today's birdwatchers would be able to pursue their hobby if it were not for the thoughtfully provided hides on reserves. The early naturalists knew how to stalk birds silently and unobtrusively just like a hunter. They knew how to take advantage of any cover, to hide behind trees, below banks, to crouch and peer through bushes and long grasses rather than over them. They camouflaged their appearance by wearing inconspicuous clothes: the brightly coloured anoraks and rustling waterproofs of today would make them wince. Above all they knew the value of patience, of being able to sit and wait. The ability to keep still and silent is rare in this noisy, urgent world, but it pays dividends when birdwatching. Slowly, as you blend into the background, the birds which perhaps flew off a little way at your approach, will return and resume their business and then you can settle down to watch them properly.

If you have only recently started birdwatching much of your note-taking *may* be devoted to writing rapid but detailed descriptions of birds and looking them up in a field guide afterwards (it is certainly an excellent exercise!), but in practice you will probably feel happier to take the field guide out with you. In either case, really get to know your field guide – the symbols and keys, and especially the order in which the birds are presented, so that instead of aimlessly and desperately flicking through the pages, you can go straight to the section on ducks or waders or warblers, as necessary.

To begin with, you will need a good view of a bird to be certain of your identification. It takes practice to be able to recognize a bird simply by the pattern of its tail feathers, or by the way it flies, so don't be discouraged if many of your birds are simply too distant or fly away too rapidly for you to identify them. Birdwatching is like any other skill; you have to start with a good basic foundation of knowledge and then build on it. Once you know the common birds of your area, you will be able to sort out the less familiar species with greater confidence and accuracy.

Look at every bird you see systematically – analyzing it according to size, shape, markings, behaviour and song.

Size can be misleading, so try to compare an unknown bird with something nearby of a known size. Then look at its general shape. You will soon learn the silhouettes that indicate some sort of duck, finch, wader or bird of prey. Within the overall impression, try to make a note of features: the shape of the wings, for example – are they long, thin, broad, fingered or pointed? The tail – is it forked, square, rounded or diamond-shaped? The bill – is it long, thin, curved, hooked, short, broad, pointed or blunt? The legs – are they long or short, set forward or back on the body?

Colour is also deceptive, changing with the light and the bird's state of moult. A field guide can only give an indication of a bird's colour pattern. Much more reliable are field marks, such as the conspicuous flashes on wings or tails. Remember that crests and other ornamental plumage may only be present during the breeding season.

Behaviour can be an excellent guide to identification. How a bird stands or moves, the way it feeds and flies can be as distinctive as a person's characteristic shrug of the shoulders, or his manner of walking. So try to notice how a bird moves, whether it walks slowly, runs or hops, whether it flies in a straight line or in an undulating fashion. Watch how and where it feeds, for example by probing the earth, or in flight, or by wading in water or diving into it.

Songs and calls are difficult to note down, and rarely bear any resemblance to the descriptions given in guides, but they can be a useful reminder, especially if you can liken them to another familiar sound, such as a squeaky gate.

Learn the correct terms for groups of feathers, so that you will understand published descriptions and be able to write accurate ones yourself.

Whether you choose to write descriptions or make quick field sketches in your notebook is up to you. A field sketch does not have to be artistic – a crude drawing based on circles and egg shapes can get the message across quickly. Some people go to the lengths of having bird outlines drawn into their notebooks in advance, but these can be misleading – imagine trying to adapt a shape drawn to suit a warbler for a wader!

At first you will be preoccupied with identifying the species of bird you are seeing, but as you gain experience you will find that it is often possible to differentiate male from female, and young birds from adults. With gulls and some birds of prey, which take several years to reach adulthood, the ability to age birds can be taken a step further.

Some birdwatchers systematically count all the birds they see; others simply make a point of recording unusually large or small numbers. Counting birds is a skill which is far from easy to acquire. With such mobile subjects, moving rapidly in large numbers, it is not always possible to count every individual, so an estimate has to be made. It is easy to become confused when counting a flock in flight, so look for a tree or other landmark they must pass and count them as they cross it. First count off ten birds, then you can estimate the number of groups of ten in the flock.

The better you know the terrain, the more accurate your counts will be. You will be able to take into consideration any gulleys or troughs in the land (or islands and reedbeds on lakes) and make doubly sure you check these.

Counting birds in woodland poses special problems. Usually it means an early start to the day if you want to hear the males singing. Spot counts can be made by stopping at roughly equidistant points within the wood, waiting for five minutes and counting the birds that can be heard or seen. A more accurate method of assessing woodland bird populations has been devised by the British Trust for Ornithology. The Common Birds Census involves using special maps provided by the BTO to plot the bird territories on the chosen study area.

To be allowed to look through a birdwatcher's field notes is always a privilege. They provide a glimpse into someone else's perception and for that reason are always individual. Some concentrate on certain species or groups, others will be quick to record displays, while yet others will make a point of looking at plants and insects and other areas of wildlife. To see how different people can be, try comparing your notes with a friend's at the end of a day in the field.

No-one can lay down hard and fast rules about what you ought to record. At the beginning of each new entry it's a good idea to record the date and possibly the time, the place (a grid reference can be useful), habitat, prevailing weather conditions, wind direction and strength. After that, it's entirely up to you. Just open your eyes and ears, and enjoy the birds and the countryside!

Equipment

To be a good birdwatcher, you need to invest not so much money as time. A vast amount of equipment is not required and most birdwatchers would rather save for a good birdwatching trip than the latest kind of telescope.

A notebook and pencil are the first essentials. Some notebooks have oilskin covers which are water repellent and therefore much more robust for use in poor weather. You will find that a pencil is more reliable and more suitable for making sketches than a ballpoint pen, and a propelling pencil can save you the bother of carrying a sharpener or several pencils. Some birdwatchers find a pocket dictaphone useful for taking rapid field notes.

As for binoculars, the most expensive need not necessarily be the best. Invest in a good pair, look after them carefully, have them serviced regularly and they should last you a lifetime. Prices range from about £40 to £400. Always try out as many pairs of binoculars as you can because it is important to find binoculars which suit *you* – that *you* find easy to handle and hold steady, and are convenient to carry.

Don't be misled into thinking that higher magnifications will make it easier to identify birds. A magnification of 7x – 10x is adequate for most birdwatching – higher than that and binoculars tend to become heavy and difficult to hold steady, and have too small a field of view. Ladies may anyway prefer something lighter, while people who wear spectacles may like to examine those with rubber eyecups which can be folded back so that the field of view is not too restricted.

Roof prism binoculars are more compact, smaller and lighter than the more traditional design. They also tend to be more expensive. Today there is a fashion for very small, lightweight binoculars. The optics are usually superb, but some people find them difficult to use simply because they are so small – bear in mind that cold winter weather makes gloved hands clumsy.

The sort of birdwatching you do will influence your choice of binoculars. If much of your birdwatching involves looking over wide stretches of water, binoculars with a larger magnification (10x or 12x) will probably be more useful, but if you are birdwatching in woodland a smaller magnification, 7x or 8x with a correspondingly wider field of view and closer focussing, should serve you better. Go to a specialist shop and take your time. Take the glasses outside and check them for brightness and clarity of colour, watch for 'fringes' of colour round subjects, and distortion of straight lines.

How about a telescope? Remember, it's a great advantage to travel light, so before buying a telescope, make sure you need one. Some people never acquire the knack of using a telescope effectively. The choice is more limited than with binoculars, but they are made with either zoom or fixed focus; prismatic or with draw-tubes. A telescope can be very useful if you do a great deal of seawatching or wildfowl watching. You will also need a tripod to hold it steady and this inevitably adds to the bulk and weight you will have to carry.

To sum up, a notebook and pencil, binoculars, and possibly a telescope – that is your basic birdwatching equipment. Later on, as your interest grows, you may decide to specialize and this may mean you have to buy some extra equipment. Most birdwatchers already own a camera and even if they do not have the skill and patience or the powerful lenses necessary for taking aesthetically pleasing bird pictures, they find a camera is extremely useful for taking 'record' shots. Dedicated bird photographers will probably need more than one camera body, an array of flashlights, lenses and an endless supply of film. A small, portable, camouflaged hide can also be useful for the natural history photographer as well as for the ornithologist making a detailed study of one particular bird.

Some birdwatchers find that sound recording adds an extra dimension to their hobby, and others take their field sketches a step further by bringing paints and brushes with them. Those who join a ringing group will need to invest in nets, rings and scales.

Lastly, don't forget that a well stocked birdtable, a small pond or birdbath and possibly a nestbox or two will work wonders in bringing birds closer to you.

Further information

Binoculars and telescopes See survey in *British Birds,* April 1985. Leaflet available from Charles Frank Ltd, PO Box 5, Ronald Lane, Saxmundham, Suffolk IP17 2NL.

Bird photography See *The Focal Guide to Bird Photography* by Michael W. Richards.

Sound recording Leaflet available from RSPB.

Sketching See *Drawing Birds* by John Busby (RSPB, due autumn 1986).

Bird ringing See BTO Guide 16.

Garden bird equipment See RSPB gift catalogue.

For lists of stockists see *The Birdwatcher's Directory* at the end of the book.

Your Own Patch

There is no better place to study birds than your own area. Every place, even a large city, is worth exploring for its birdlife, and by getting to know your local and common birds thoroughly you will give yourself an excellent grounding for more wide-ranging activities later. Most of today's top ornithologists began in that way, spending many hours during their childhood watching the birds on their own local patch.

Birdwatching can easily be combined with other activities: the daily walk with the dog, fishing, horse-riding, even the journey into work (but do take care if you are driving!). Get into the habit of opening your eyes and ears to the birdlife around you wherever you happen to be and you will be well rewarded. Your senses will soon become sharper.

First of all, obtain a large-scale Ordnance Survey map of the area you want to study. Examine if carefully, marking the places that you already know are good for birds, and looking for those which could be promising. Here the keyword is 'edge': places where several habitats converge are likely to be especially rich in birdlife. For example, the corner of a field, flanked by a hedge on one side, with a wood on the other and a pond on the far side of the hedge. An area of water will always attract birds.

Having decided on a suitable study area, the next thing to do is to make a thorough survey of it. Pay particular attention to the types of habitat and vegetation. Try to identify the plants and trees and note their relative heights. Think in terms of what sort of nesting sites they can offer and the food they provide for birds. This should give you some good clues to the bird species you can expect to see. With successive visits you can gradually build up a picture of the bird population (keep an eye open for other creatures too) and during the breeding season you should be able to plot individual territories. Just as a gardener obtains great satisfaction in knowing his plants and shrubs as individuals, the birdwatcher can achieve a similarly intimate knowledge of the birds that share his surroundings.

Many birdwatchers use their local areas as a basis for their own participation in the Common Birds Census organized by the British Trust for Ornithology, one of the longest-running surveys of bird populations. Others embark on detailed studies of individual species or branch out to find an extra interest in the fungi, flowers or insects of their patch.

Be careful not to take on more than you can manage. Don't plan a daily ten-mile walk if it is going to be too much for you. If you enjoy no more than a gentle half-mile stroll, that is fine. You may prefer a short cycle ride or car drive to a nearby reservoir or beach. The important thing is that your chosen study area should be close enough for you to visit it frequently, if not every day then at least once or twice a month, so that in a short time you will be able to build up a good picture of the regular birdlife.

    Incidentally, although an OS map will indicate paths, it will not always show whether they are public rights of way. These can usually be checked with the county surveyor's office or the relevant parish council. If you know of some good birding patches that are on private land, or your survey 'square' would just be completed if you could take a short-cut across a particular meadow, don't hesitate to ask. If you live in a small village you will probably know the landowner personally and can request permission to make a regular survey of the birds. Otherwise, write a pleasant letter explaining who you are and what you would like to do. The worst that can happen is that the owner says no, but on the other hand he or she may be delighted that someone else appreciates their land, and this may kindle or stimulate their own interest – so you will have done your own little bit of public relations for wildlife conservation! Don't forget to follow up your good work by sending the owner annual reports of your findings.

    On the subject of reports, remember also to send your records to the county bird recorder. These records may not seem all that important in your eyes, but they should certainly help to create a more complete impression of local bird populations and movements.

    Now turn the page to start your own set of local records.

Your Own Patch

Use these pages to document your favourite birdwatching area. Draw a map on the facing page, marking significant features such as hedges and ponds and indicating songposts, habitual nesting trees, roosting sites and so on as you become aware of them. Don't forget to include a scale and the direction of North.

The spaces below are for listing local bird species and other wildlife, and need little explanation. For details of a bird's status, i.e. whether it is resident, or a summer visitor, etc, see the Life-list beginning on page 102.

BIRDS	FIRST SEEN	STATUS	BIRDS	FIRST SEEN	STATUS

OTHER WILDLIFE

PLACE

DESCRIPTION

1 SQUARE =

Bird Reserves

A reserve is by no means the only place to see birds; nor should anyone assume that they can be one hundred per cent certain of seeing the birds that are supposed to breed or winter there. With those provisos in mind, there are indeed many splendid areas, including more than 100 RSPB reserves, that are managed especially for their bird life, and many more that hold good numbers of birds while perhaps being more notable for other wildlife.

Many reserves are delightful spots in their own right; they can be savoured for their magnificent views, plants and insects. Imagine the superb dragonflies of Arne in summer, the myriad flowers of Balranald, the otters of Leighton Moss and that delicate butterfly, the heath fritillary at Church Wood, Blean in Kent. Such sights are just as memorable as the Dartford warblers, corncrakes, bitterns and marsh harriers and the nightingales which might first spring to a birdwatcher's mind.

Access to reserves managed by voluntary conservation bodies varies. Some are usually open to the general public, others restrict access to members and may admit the public only on special open days. RSPB members have free access to the Society's reserves, but in some cases, in the interests of the birds, visitors have to be limited. The moral is: do check on visiting details first. Find out whether a charge is made, or whether permits are required. This may seem tedious, but it can save a disappointment. If some of the more popular reserves were not protected, they might end up like a famous country house on a wet bank holiday – just one long queue of shuffling people – and that is definitely *not* the way to watch birds!

There is not space to give comprehensive visiting details here, but there is a list of useful addresses at the end of the book.

Many reserves have hides at particularly good vantage points, perhaps overlooking water, or raised on stilts to give a better view over a reedbed. Approach hides quietly, opening doors and windows with care and being sure to shut them when you leave. Don't push telescopes, camera lenses or hands through the slats. Many hides are approached by a covered walkway to reduce disturbance to the birds. Make use of the walkways and don't walk along the top of a bank in an attempt to get a better view: good fieldcraft is as essential on a reserve as anywhere else.

Lastly, don't be afraid to ask. Wardens are usually only too happy to spend a few minutes chatting to visitors, telling them which birds have been around over the past few days, and about breeding successes and migrants. Many go to the trouble of keeping a noticeboard listing recent sightings, so even if they and their helpers are not on hand at the time there is some up-to-date information for visitors. And, if you happen to be in the fortunate position of being an expert among beginners, don't be too shy to share your knowledge – a little help with identification may give someone else just the encouragement they need to get really involved with this marvellous hobby.

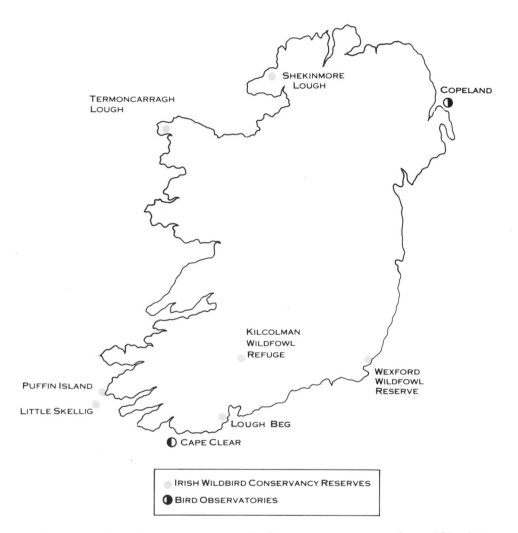

SHEKINMORE
LOUGH

COPELAND

TERMONCARRAGH
LOUGH

KILCOLMAN
WILDFOWL
REFUGE

WEXFORD
WILDFOWL
RESERVE

PUFFIN ISLAND

LITTLE SKELLIG

LOUGH BEG

CAPE CLEAR

IRISH WILDBIRD CONSERVANCY RESERVES
BIRD OBSERVATORIES

These maps show the RSPB reserves which are open to visitors, the Wildfowl Trust
Centres, Irish Wildbird Conservancy reserves, bird observatories and those
National Nature Reserves which are of particular interest for birdwatchers, plus
one or two other famous spots. You may like to add your own favourite
birdwatching areas and perhaps any reserves managed by your local naturalists'
trust.

HERMANESS

NOSS

FAIR ISLE

| BIRD OBSERVATORIES |
| DECOYS OR RINGING STATIONS |
| NATIONAL NATURE RESERVES NOTED FOR THEIR BIRD INTEREST |
| WILDFOWL CENTRES OPEN TO THE PUBLIC |

NORTH RONA
AND
SULA SGEIR

INVERPOLLY

ST. KILDA ♂

MONACH ISLES

LOCH DRUIDIBEG

RHUM

BEINN
EIGHE

NIGG AND UDALE BAYS

CRAIGELLACHIE

SANDS OF FORVIE

CAIRNGORMS

MORTON
LOCHS

TENTSMUIR POINT

LOCH
LOMOND

LOCH
LEVEN

ISLE OF MAY

LINDISFARNE

CAERLAVEROCK

WASHINGTON

CALF OF
MAN

WALNEY

AINSDALE SANDS

MARTIN
MERE

SPURN

SALTFLEETBY –
THEDDLETHORPE DUNES

NEWBOROUGH
WARREN

ROSTHERNE MERE

GIBRALTAR PT.

SCOLT HEAD
ISLAND

BARDSEY

DYFI

HOLME

HOLKHAM

CORS
TREGARON

BOROUGH FEN

PEAKIRK

WELNEY

HICKLING BROAD

BURE MARSHES

CASTOR
HANGLANDS

WESTLETON
HEATH

WALBERSWICK

SKOMER
SKOKHOLM

TRING RESERVOIRS

NACTON

ORFORDNESS-
HAVERGATE

OXWICH

SLIMBRIDGE

ABBERTON

BRAUNTON
BURROWS

HIGH HALSTOW

LEIGH

BRIDGWATER
BAY

SWALE

SANDWICH BAY

THURSLEY

ARUNDEL

STODMARSH

DUNGENESS

STUDLAND
HEATH

PORTLAND

LUMBISTER

NORTH FETLAR

LOCH OF SPIGGLE

NORTH HILL
NOUP CLIFFS
MARWICK HEAD
DALE OF COTTASGARTH
THE LOONS
HOBBISTER
NORTH HOY
COPINSAY

HANDA

● RSPB RESERVES

BALRANALD

CULBIN SANDS
LOCH OF STRATHBEG
LOCH GARTEN
INSH MARSHES
KILLIECRANKIE
LOCH OF KINNORDY
FOWLSHEUGH
VANE FARM
LOCH GRUINART
BARONS HAUGH
LOCHWINNOCH
RATHLIN ISLAND CLIFFS
LOUGH FOYLE
CASTLECALDWELL
SHANES CASTLE
KEN / DEE MARSHES
WOOD OF CREE
GREENCASTLE POINT
GELTSDALE
MULL OF GALLOWAY
ST BEES HEAD
LEIGHTON MOSS & MORECAMBE BAY
BEMPTON CLIFFS
HORNSEA MERE
EASTWOOD
BLACKTOFT SANDS
FAIRBURN INGS
SOUTH STACK CLIFFS
POINT OF AYR
TETNEY MARSHES
GAYTON SANDS
COOMBES VALLEY
TITCHWELL MARSH
COED GARTH GELL
LAKE VYRNWY
NENE WASHES
SNETTISHAM
YNYS-HIR
STRUMPSHAW FEN & SURLINGHAM MARSH
SANDWELL VALLEY
MINSMERE
OUSE WASHES
WYE/ELAN
THE LODGE
NORTH WARREN
DINAS/ GWENFFRWD
FOWLMERE
HAVERGATE ISLAND
WOLVES WOOD
GRASSHOLM
NAGSHEAD
RYE HOUSE MARSH
STOUR WOOD
CWM CLYDACH
OLD HALL MARSHES
CHURCH WOOD
ELMLEY MARSHES
CHAPEL WOOD
WEST SEDGEMOOR
NORTHWARD HILL
CHURCH WOOD, BLEAN
BARFOLD COPSE
AYLESBEARE COMMON
LANGSTONE HARBOUR
DUNGENESS
ARNE
FORE WOOD
RADIPOLE & LODMOOR

Weather Conditions

One of the first things a birdwatcher will put in his notebook alongside the date and place will be the weather conditions. Although prevailing rain or sunshine may well influence bird behaviour, general weather trends over the previous few days may have a more significant effect.

High winds and storms, especially at peak migration times, can mean that birds are blown off course and that there is a good chance of seeing either an unusual foreign visitor or seabirds that have been blown inland. In winter, long periods of very low temperatures will prompt mass movements of birds searching for food. Flocks of waterfowl may congregate in thousands on one day, and the following day most will be gone. Inland waterbirds such as kingfishers, herons and coots are prompted to move to the coast in search of unfrozen feeding grounds, and flocks of thrushes and lapwings roam the countryside. In the very hard winter of 1981–82, 13,000 lapwings were counted moving in a south-westerly direction over Radipole in Dorset, fleeing before yet another approaching snowstorm. Small, insectivorous birds like wrens and goldcrests are badly affected by freezing weather, and die in large numbers. Fortunately, although their populations may be drastically reduced, small birds are usually able to recover their numbers quickly, in the space of a few years.

Very cold weather combined with shorter periods of daylight means that birds spend most of their time feeding. They tend to have a rounder, plumper appearance than in summer, because they fluff up their feathers to give better insulation against the cold. Still, they can lose valuable body heat through their feet and bills, so when roosting they tuck their bills under their wings or shoulder feathers, and draw up one leg. Even so, waders seem to fall victim to frostbite, for they sometimes lose toes or parts of their feet. In snow, birds such as moorhens, coots and blackbirds can all be seen crouching down whenever they stop to cover both legs with feathers.

Communal roosting is another way birds attempt to keep warm during cold winter nights. Starlings form huge roosts, often in town centres, where the temperatures are probably one or two degrees higher than out in the country. Wrens and long-tailed tits literally snuggle up together – once no fewer than 64 wrens were found in a nestbox! Many birds, in fact, use nestboxes and old nests as roost-sites, and blue tits have been seen roosting in the warmth of street lamps.

In spring, a prolonged or sudden snap of cold and wet weather can mean disaster for early broods, especially for waders and ducks, whose nests may be flooded out or whose chicks become chilled in long, wet grass. Sometimes wardens on tern reserves have to resort to moving vulnerable nests higher up the beach to try and prevent them from being flooded by abnormally high tides.

Bird species react in various ways to the weather. For example, few birds will sing in rain, but one notable exception is the mistle thrush, whose other name, stormcock, betrays this tendency. High winds also create problems for many birds and they seem to fly only when they really need to, with laboured, almost desperate, wingbeats. Other birds such as crows, ravens and choughs seem to revel in playing on the wind, while fulmars and gannets are virtually disdainful of the elements.

A bright sunny day is much more likely to induce birds to sing and an unusually warm day in mid-winter may tempt blackbirds and robins to give voice. A clear night with a bright moon can encourage birds to sing and robins have been known to sing in the depths of night, bathed in the light of a street lamp.

In sheltered spots in gardens and parks you may notice birds sunbathing. They stretch out their wings and raise their back feathers, sometimes they seem to pant as well. It is thought that sunlight helps birds to manufacture vitamin D, but it may also reduce infestation by parasites. Some species such as sparrows like to dustbathe in clear fine weather. Too much sun, on the other hand, can be bad for birds – eggs and nestlings may need to be shielded against overheating.

Generally, heavy rain reduces birds' feeding activity, although some birds are happy to bathe in rain and it is quite a common sight to see pigeons and doves with one wing raised as they enjoy a quick shower. Small birds like warblers may rub against the large, dew-covered leaves of cabbages to have a bath. A period of drought will ensure that garden birdbaths, man-made ponds and even lawn sprinklers and hoses suddenly become extremely popular with birds. As with frost, drought means that the ground can become too hard for some birds to feed. Blackbirds can no longer feed on worms which retreat into the depths of the soil, and starlings cannot probe the lawn for leatherjackets, while song thrushes find that the supply of garden snails has literally dried up.

Birds that feed on insects which they catch in flight are indirectly influenced by air pressure and temperature for these factors affect the height at which insects fly. For example, spotted flycatchers tend to feed in the tree canopy early and late in the day, catching midges and aphids, but during the late morning and afternoon, when larger flying insects are to be found nearer the ground, they use comparatively low perches.

Spotted flycatchers, along with many insectivorous species, make certain of a continuous food supply during our winter by migrating south to Africa. When birds undertake these major journeys, they are reacting in a most dramatic way to prevailing weather conditions. We look at patterns of migration on the following pages.

Migration

Despite years of scientific research, how and why birds migrate are questions that have been answered only partially. That they undertake long journeys in search of food is generally accepted, but the initial cause of such movements may have been in response to changing climates and successive ice ages.

The instinctive urge to travel north or south is probably triggered off by changes in the hours of daylight. We know that the positions of the sun and stars influence navigation, that fog can disorientate migrating birds, and that a response to the earth's magnetic field may also play a part. Thanks to recoveries of ringed birds, we also have detailed knowledge of where many of our birds spent the winter or summer.

When we think of migrating birds we tend to think first of the summer migrants – birds that come to Britain to breed and spend three or four months here. The annual arrival of swallows, swifts and house martins is eagerly awaited and welcomed by everyone; but they, of course, are by no means the only migrants.

In fact, very few birds are faithful to the same territory throughout the year. Birds of the same species may be nearly always present in an area, but not the same individuals. In some instances the summer-breeding birds are replaced by more northerly ones in winter. This is thought to be what happens with overwintering blackcaps. British robins (especially the males) are fairly sedentary, but the females have to find separate territories for the winter and may be forced to cross the English Channel. Scandinavian robins, on the other hand, are definitely migratory. Thousands of European birds, such as skylarks, lapwings and starlings, also join our resident birds during the winter months, but when we think of winter migrants it is usually of the huge numbers of geese, ducks and swans that seek refuge on our small island. It is just as moving and magical a sight to watch the greylag geese arriving from Iceland, or Bewick's swans planing in from Siberia, as it is to find that the swallows have once again taken up residence in the barn.

As well as the summer and winter visitors, there are passage migrants – birds such as whimbrels and curlew sandpipers – which may stop off briefly before flying on. In some years large numbers of birds arrive in areas where they are not normally seen. Waxwings are well known for such 'irruptions'. Occasionally bad weather results in a 'fall' of migrants, when the birds are literally forced to the ground by strong winds. The species most commonly affected tend to be small ones such as goldcrests, warblers and flycatchers.

The migrants we mostly see are day-flying landbirds, but many species (notably thrushes) migrate at night. Seabirds, too, migrate. Razorbills and guillemots tend to stay near the continental shelf, whereas puffins, shearwaters and gannets roam far and wide.

In winter, bird populations are usually more fluid and mobile, moving according to the availability of food. You may see flocks of lapwings regularly feeding in one field for several weeks; then they move to an adjacent pasture or perhaps leave the district entirely. Many birds find safety in numbers and feed in flocks with other species outside the breeding season, so it is always worth checking flocks carefully to see how they are made up. Chaffinches and bramblings often feed together; so do lapwings and golden plovers. Fieldfare and redwings can be seen alongside blackbirds, and a flock of winter gulls may harbour an Iceland gull or a glaucous gull.

As well as the seasonal migrations that take place, birds will make daily flights between their roosting and feeding grounds. It can be interesting to time the evening fly-past of gulls, for example, returning from a day's foraging at the local rubbish tip. By watching birds flying past at dawn and dusk you will be able to get an idea of their regular flightpaths.

If you want to watch birds migrating, much will depend on local geography. There are certain narrow stretches of land or promontories famous for being good places from which to watch birds on migration. Often they are the sites of bird observatories, such as Portland Bill. Some birdwatchers go to Gibraltar or the Bosporus especially to watch the autumn passage of migrants, particularly raptors. By understanding the geography of your own area, you will soon get to know the ridges and corners that attract migrants or offer a good vantage point.

Many birdwatchers keep an annual note of when they see their first swallow, wheatear, chiffchaff, etc, but it is also an interesting exercise to find out exactly when they leave. You will need to keep a close watch on the regular birds in your area towards the time they are due to leave, and make a note each day you hear or see them – until one day your diary is empty.

You will find your skill at counting flocks (see 'How To Take Field Notes') comes into play when studying migrating birds. As well as making a particular note of the direction and speed of the wind, and cloud cover, you should try to record the species you see, any flight calls, the direction of flight and the height at which the birds are flying, and the numbers passing over.

Observatories

A goldcrest alights briefly on a coastal gorse bush, then makes a determined dart for another. In mid-air it stops, flutters briefly and hangs softly, unmoving, suspended in mid-air. In fact it is trapped in a net so fine as to be almost invisible.

Seconds later a hand deftly scoops the bird out of the net pocket. The fragile creature is popped into a small cotton bag and weighed, then measured. The figures are noted down. Then the observatory warden selects a small band of metal and, holding the bird in one hand, he slips the ring around the bird's leg, securing it with a special pair of pliers so that it will neither slip off nor impede the bird's movement. The warden releases his grip on the goldcrest which lies still for a moment, allowing onlookers to marvel at its delicate plumage, its bright black eye, its very smallness. Then it flits away. It preens for a little while on a bush, then it is gone, continuing its autumn journey inland. The whole process has taken only a few minutes.

The bird observatories that are scattered about Britain's coastline (see maps on pages 23-24) are run by the Bird Observatories Council under the aegis of the British Trust for Ornithology. Several times a year bird-ringing courses are held at observatories, and at other times birdwatchers are welcome to stay and help. A visit to an observatory gives an excellent chance to understand a little more about ringing, which is particularly useful in the study of migration. The recovery of ringed birds enables ornithologists to find out the routes they take and where they spend the rest of the year. In addition, ringing provides information on mortality rates. (If you find a dead bird which has been ringed, send the ring to the British Trust for Ornithology at Tring (see 'The Birdwatcher's Directory') with the date and circumstances of its recovery. In return you will receive details of where and when the bird was ringed.)

For many birdwatchers the main attraction of going to an observatory is the very real possibility of seeing an unusual migrant, because observatories are generally situated on projecting spurs or tiny islands which are the first available landing point for birds that have crossed a large stretch of water.

As well as seeing mist nets in use, you may see

birds driven through a Heligoland trap, which has a very wide entrance, narrowing through a net funnel to a point where the bird is caught. Sometimes groups of ringers go out to ring waders at high tide, using cannon nets. To ensure that birds are not subjected to stress, ringing may only be carried out under licence. If you would like to know more, contact the British Trust for Ornithology.

Generally, members of the public are welcome at observatories, but if you are planning on staying or wish to bring a large party, make arrangements with the warden first.

Birdwatching Actively

For many people the attraction of birdwatching lies in its being a relatively solitary pursuit. Those who enjoy peace and solitude may not take kindly to organized birdwatching outings or group activities, but welcome the chance to inject more purpose into their hobby by taking part in some of the surveys run by the RSPB, BTO or Young Ornithologists' Club.

Some, such as the YOC's Migrant Arrival Phone-In, may involve just a simple telephone call to report your sightings (details are given annually in the YOC's magazine, *Bird Life*). Others require a more serious commitment, with regular surveys and information cards to be completed. For many, the advantage of partaking in a survey is that it gives them a little extra incentive and ensures that they actually get out to watch birds from time to time.

For example, if you live near the coast, you could take part in the RSPB's Beached Bird Survey, which helps to monitor the effects of oil pollution. Another coastal project, jointly organized by the RSPB, BTO and Nature Conservancy Council, is the Birds of Estuaries Enquiry which relies on volunteers making monthly counts at major sites. Wader enthusiasts may also be interested in the Wader Study Group Projects.

The Wildfowl Trust organizes several surveys and counts, but the major co-ordinator of studies by amateur birdwatchers is the BTO. Apart from the Common Birds Census, it supervises a number of other important projects. The Garden Bird Feeding Survey has been running since 1970. It depends on a group of 200 participants providing a great deal of information about birds that come to take food during the winter. The Waterways Birds Survey concentrates on monitoring riparian birds, while the Nest Record Scheme gathers facts on the breeding biology of birds, collecting data on the number of eggs laid, young reared and the effects of weather and predation. In addition, the BTO organized the collation of material for the *Atlas of Breeding Birds of Britain and Ireland,* and more recently, the *Winter Atlas,* which will be based on the distribution of birds in Britain and Ireland during the winter.

It also arranges for regular surveys of the populations of several bird species such as herons, rooks and mute swans, and is compiling a Register of Ornithological Sites.

For more information about current projects, consult the appropriate society or the *Birdwatcher's Yearbook.* You will see that the enthusiastic birdwatcher need never be bored or at a loss for a way to make his or her own positive and valuable contribution to ornithology.

Field Notes

Over to you! These are the pages for your own field notes, pages on which you can pay tribute to those special days when the birds were good. And by 'good' we don't necessarily mean rarities or exotic vagrants, but the circumstances perhaps where the birds, the light and the scenery combine to make an unforgettable moment. It may be distant views of geese on a wild, wintry day; flocks of starlings wheeling in to roost; the lightning strike of a sparrowhawk in the garden or the sudden flurry of squabbling coots – anything, in fact, which you would like to transcribe from your rough notes.

These pages have been designed with a minimum of rules and headings so they can be adapted to suit your own requirements. You may be good at drawing and like to make lots of sketches, or you may feel happier writing out your descriptions. Whatever your preference, you can use these pages in a variety of ways – on one day counting a large flock, on another noting an interesting piece of behaviour, or making detailed notes on identification. The choice is yours.

In between your personal pages we have included some examples of other birdwatchers' notes of outings, holidays and studies. Their impressions will give you a flavour of several habitats and places – not all of them bird reserves – and show you a variety of approaches for your own notes.

Field Notes

DATE	TIME
PLACE	

. . . .

WEATHER CONDITIONS

. . . .

WIND DIRECTION

NOTES OR SKETCHES

DATE	TIME

PLACE

WEATHER CONDITIONS

WIND DIRECTION

NOTES OR SKETCHES

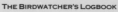

DATE	TIME

PLACE

WEATHER CONDITIONS

WIND DIRECTION

NOTES OR SKETCHES

DATE	TIME

PLACE

WEATHER CONDITIONS

WIND DIRECTION

NOTES OR SKETCHES

Summer And Skylarks

Here are two versions of the same outing. The first shows the kind of data to jot down in your notebook as you go, and the second is a fuller descriptive account, recalled in the tranquillity of evening.

Date: 18 June.
Place: usual walk – Wimpole Rd, Eversden (Cambridgeshire).
Time: 5 pm.
Weather: very warm; no cloud, sky bright blue.
Wind direction: very calm.

Pigs' field
4 magpies incl 2 juvs
6 jackdaws
3 rooks
5 turtle doves
c30 house sparrows
5 yellowhammers (2 m) ⎤
3 greenfinches   ⎦ feeding together
wren scolding in hedge
cuckoo
3 swallows hawking in lane,
but NB – flying v high

Farmyard
French partridge

Bridlepath
2 woodpigeons flying towards copse
1 pheasant – alarm call from copse
3 corn buntings – all singing from usual songposts
skylarks everywhere!

RAH.

THE BIRDWATCHER'S LOGBOOK

Cambridgeshire farmland. Mid-June.
Late afternoon: very warm, no cloud, calm.

This is prairieland and amongst the rolling acres of corn the field of pigs draws birds like a magnet, so it is always worthwhile including this on my route. The magpies are there, with two young ones with short tails, and several jackdaws. Their combined garrulous chattering, plus the rooks' more restrained occasional caws, the sparrows' chirruping and the pigs' snuffling grunts combine to make this a noisy as well as somewhat noisome half-acre!

All the crows are quite wary and keep their distance. Typically, the magpies will bounce off Indian-file and lurk behind the farm buildings. The sparrows get up with a great dust-flying whirr but quickly return to glean any discarded grains and seeds from the floor. Amongst them are a few greenfinches and two or three yellowhammers – how vividly yellow and chestnut are the males! In summer this is usually a good spot for turtle doves and today there are five of them. I always marvel at their diamond-spangled backs and brilliant white tail feathers. They breed in the spinney, along with the magpies, long-tailed tits and no doubt a host of other small birds.

A bird has been sitting on the telegraph wire. Now it flies and calls 'cuckoo' – I should have noticed it before! Swallows hawk over the field and occasionally dive to twist and turn the length of the lane, but generally they are flying very high today.

Walking past the farmyard, I suddenly notice a partridge – French variety. It sees me too; freezes, then slowly sinks and crouches on the concrete, trying, painfully, to be invisible. I move on, and let it imagine the ruse has worked!

Towards the hill, ignoring the wood pigeons commuting between the copses, I look for the corn buntings. There is a male to almost every songpost – bushes are sparse along the track. They call and sing their funny, jangly song and allow me to come very close before flying off, feet trailing. I feel quite affectionate towards these dumpy little birds – they are *so* predictable that I am sure I know each one.

Pulling up the hill towards the stunning gold square of rape that stands between the barley and wheat, I look hopefully for kestrels. They should be plentiful, but I've only ever seen one here. In front of me the skylarks rise indignantly; sweeping upwards as if drawn by an invisible thread. I reach the brow of the hill and turn back to admire the view – seven miles and more into Cambridge. Through binoculars I can even pick out individual buildings. The sky above is a vivid, almost continental blue and cloudless; the air overflows with the rich, tumbling trill of skylarks, too high to see. At moments like this everything seems right with life.

S.M.S

Field Notes

DATE	TIME

PLACE

WEATHER CONDITIONS

WIND DIRECTION

NOTES OR SKETCHES

Date	Time

Place

Weather Conditions

Wind Direction

Notes or Sketches

DATE	TIME

PLACE

WEATHER CONDITIONS

WIND DIRECTION

NOTES OR SKETCHES

DATE	TIME

PLACE

WEATHER CONDITIONS

WIND DIRECTION

NOTES OR SKETCHES

Welsh Woodland

Ynys-hir, Dyfed. May.

Arrived in the car park at 7.00 am. The sun had long since risen above the hills bordering the southern edge of the Dyfi estuary and the valley was bathed in a warm, bright light. It promised to be a fine spring day.

The weather over the past few days had been good for migration and the main oakwood was alive with the urgent calls of newly arrived summer visitors. It was there I went first, following the marked trails that weaved through the oak trees and sun-dappled clearings. There were birds everywhere. Chiffchaffs bounced their repetitive song around the half-opened canopy and willow warblers flitted through the understorey chasing the first insects of the day. Blackcaps and garden warblers were singing loudly from bramble patches and dense ivy cover. (These two species have a similar song and after a year's absence I need to spend some time sorting them out. Blackcaps are supposed to sing in shorter bursts than garden warblers, but with the first rush of spring fever this textbook rule is often forgotten.)

As I walked along the trail, pied flycatchers became more frequent. The majority of birds were males; the females were yet to arrive. These birds were very active, some dropping down to the ground or shooting up to the treetops after insects, others busily inspecting nestboxes or chasing off other males, all the time calling their hard, short 'pwitt' and flicking their black and white wings.

By comparison, the redstarts proved more elusive. Several times I heard their thin, scratchy song but each time I failed to find the songster before it moved on. Eventually, as I crossed over the ridge on to the steeper side of the wood, there was a flash of chestnut in a clearing and there sat a fine male, upright and alert, with tail quivering.

I watched the bird until a new sound tugged me away. This was a loud but gentle 'tue' repeated two or three times and then, after a short gap, a descending trill ending in a slight flourish. The source of the sound was moving slowly through the lower branches and was not difficult to find – a striking yellow and green wood warbler. On this steeper side of the wood the bramble and bracken gave way to a more open, grassy floor carpeted with bluebells. This habitat is preferred by wood warblers and as I dropped down to the wood's edge, I encountered another three.

Moving out of the wood I came into a ride running between the wood edge and an area of birch scrub. The sun had yet to reach this spot but there were still some birds on the move, including my first willow tit of the day. Shortly after this a loud 'kek kek kek' burst into the air as a lesser spotted woodpecker bounded overhead.

The end of the ride opened out onto West Marsh, a large area of bog, reedbed and willow scrub. The bushes there were full of more willow warblers and chiffchaffs, probably freshly arrived the night before. From a tall Scot's pine a tree pipit launched itself into the bright morning air, only to drop back again on outstretched wings, singing its equally bright song.

From the depths of a bramble patch a grasshopper warbler purred constantly, impossible to see, so I turned my attention to a fine male whinchat feeding along a barbed wire fence.

It was tempting to linger in the warm sun, with the birds around me active and singing, and high above, a buzzard turning lazy circles. However, out on the estuary the tide was rising and the distant calls of redshank and curlew urged me to press on. If I could reach the hide on the edge of the estuary in time, I should be treated to a fly-past of all the waders as they moved up to their high-tide roost.

With the day just beginning, there was still much to see.

S.R

Field Notes

DATE	TIME

PLACE

WEATHER CONDITIONS

WIND DIRECTION

NOTES OR SKETCHES

DATE	TIME

PLACE

WEATHER CONDITIONS

WIND DIRECTION

NOTES OR SKETCHES

DATE	TIME

PLACE

WEATHER CONDITIONS

WIND DIRECTION

NOTES OR SKETCHES

DATE	TIME

PLACE

WEATHER CONDITIONS

WIND DIRECTION

NOTES OR SKETCHES

Roost In The Reedbeds

Leighton Moss, Lancashire. Early September.
A glorious calm, sunny day after several days of unsettled weather. The light from the YOC hide was superb, with the evening sun highlighting the bronze reedheads of the full grown reed.

A careful count of the wildfowl gave 472 mallard, mainly on the water or on the piles of reed that had been cut as 'loafing areas'. The 92 teal were scattered throughout the areas of thin marestail growth. Most of the teal and mallard were resting, but almost all the 48 shoveler were actively feeding, sieving the water with their spatulate bills and often describing circles on the calm water as they fed in small groups. The nine gadwall were upending, revealing their white underparts – such a good field mark. Most wildfowl were still in eclipse, although several mallard showed some signs of full plumage. The calm rhythm of activity would be

suddenly broken by groups of teal starting to bathe, splashing vigorously and even at times rushing across the water and making headlong dives. This activity appeared infectious and more teal and some mallard would join in.

The first small flock of starlings headed across the sky making for the field to the south which is one of their favourite pre-roost gathering areas. Up to 150 swallows and 20 sand martins hawked over the mere.

A search of the willows within the reedbed revealed two male sparrowhawks, both perched on dead branches just below the crown of the bush, waiting in ambush.

Suddenly, about 50 mallard all started moving towards the reed edge, and assembled in a rough semi-circle facing the reeds. At first I could not locate their focus of attention, but then a bittern appeared at the fringe of the reeds and worked its way slowly from clump to clump with neck extended towards the water. After about five minutes it paused, made a quick lunge and caught a small eel, then slowly withdrew into the reeds to deal with its food in privacy. Three greenshanks circled the pool calling loudly, looking for suitable feeding areas, but, finding none, headed towards the shallower West Mere.

Starlings were now arriving in strength. Large flocks which had assembled elsewhere joined together so that there were perhaps 10,000 birds moving first up the valley, then turning in unison as they reached the edge of the reedbed, then back again. As they passed the hide, a female sparrowhawk appeared and flew up towards the flock, quickly followed by another. The effect was electrifying. The whole flock rose higher and as the sparrowhawks approached, the starlings twisted and turned in their thousands, producing an amazing rippling effect like animated smoke, the ripple quickly passing through the whole flock then back again, and all the time the starlings tried to keep above the sparrowhawks, both of which made several rather half-hearted attempts to separate birds from the flock. After a short time, one and then the other broke off the encounter and drifted slowly away.

A few moments later the flock started towards the reeds. At the critical moment, as the first birds were about to land, a female sparrowhawk swept over, singled out a starling and quickly flew it down, taking it in flight in her talons. Then with the starlings squealing in terror, she flew across the pool to alight on a pile of cut reeds in full view. She started to pluck the now limp form and, like the bittern before, attracted an audience of mallard. The starlings rose once more after this successful ambush, but quickly started to drop into the reeds again, this time selecting a different area.

Two male sparrowhawks now launched their attacks, passing low over the reeds then through the descending masses of starlings, which responded by rising and twisting as onc body. This seemed to confuse the sparrowhawks and despite the abundance of birds they missed several times before one at least was successful and flew with heavy, labouring flight out of sight behind the willows. The female was still plucking, but suddenly something startled her and she flew off with her prey and headed for the woods.

By now only a few late-comers were rushing headlong into the roost. My final 'guesstimate' was about 25,000 starlings, including two semi-albinos.

A constant stream of swallows had been arriving from the coast. There had obviously been a large migration that day, no doubt taking advantage of the fine weather. They stretched across the valley and many were singing, adding to the chorus of the roosting starlings. Several hundred swallows mobbed a sparrowhawk as it headed away from the starling roost. Suddenly all the swallows stopped feeding and rose several hundred feet, moving up the valley until even in binoculars they appeared like a mass of swarming insects. Then they dropped back, rushed in at low level and quickly settled down into the reeds at the edge of the mere, not far from the roosting starlings.

The evening spectacular was over. I walked home in the dusk, noting several noctule bats hawking moths, while the first tawny owl started to call.

J.W

Field Notes

DATE	**TIME**

PLACE

WEATHER CONDITIONS

WIND DIRECTION

NOTES OR SKETCHES

DATE	TIME

PLACE

WEATHER CONDITIONS

WIND DIRECTION

NOTES OR SKETCHES

DATE	TIME
PLACE	

WEATHER CONDITIONS

WIND DIRECTION

NOTES OR SKETCHES

DATE	TIME

PLACE

WEATHER CONDITIONS

WIND DIRECTION

NOTES OR SKETCHES

Wild Geese In Their Thousands

Islay. Early March.
Weather: very changeable, from gales and rain to sunshine.
Loch Gruinart, a long, broad inlet into the north coast of Islay, lay silver and serene, edged with bright ochre-yellow where the sun caught the banks of sand at low tide. The calls of choughs, thin and tinny with distance, penetrated the lochside dunes. Out on the flats were geese – 500 barnacles, returned to their roost-site after being disturbed from their early-morning feed.

I drove round the head of the loch across the rushy, wet fields of Gruinart Flats. There were far more geese here – perhaps 3,000 barnacles, all beautiful and clean-cut, in handsome black, white, grey and cream. Some were scarcely forty yards off – with a telescope I could see every feather of their dense, velvety plumage, with the healthy bloom of geese in good condition, fattening up for their long journey north. Some bigger, dark brown geese – Greenland white-fronts – were scattered near the field edge, keeping to the cover of rank rushes. Perfect blue-black and white rock doves sped by. Suddenly there was alarm amongst the geese – across the flats a great bird was floating like a giant harrier, wings up in a V as it tilted from side to side, searching the edge of the heather moor. A golden eagle was down from the hills, looking for hares.

I crossed to Loch Indaal, now very calm and bright after the previous day's gales. Great northern diver, long-tailed duck and eiders added variety, but the chief interest was the flock of scaup – 485, with 200 of them very close in, the drakes calling with piping, bubbling notes between tufted duck and pochard in tone, the ducks growling. Nearby were red-breasted mergansers, a whooper swan and choughs.

Back to Gruinart Farm – another 1,000-plus barnacles here. Two hen harriers too, and a buzzard. Driving through broken ground, patched with heather and small grassy fields, I came across small groups of Greenland white-fronts – 20, 50, 37, then 93. There were several hundred more barnacles as well, another hen harrier, and in a field with white-fronts and common gulls, two superb first-year Iceland gulls!

Weaving back to another part of Loch Indaal, another 1,500 barnacles and 120 white-fronts were joined by a pink-footed goose, with eight Slavonian grebes out on the loch.

A magical spell started with a golden eagle spotted up ahead. I stopped and watched as the great bird – a young one – passed within 200 yards before settling on a rock. Gulls chased it, and when it perched a hooded crow crept up behind and actually pecked its tail! Another big raptor was soaring beyond it – it took 10–15 seconds to swing round in a wide, circling glide, showing the steadiness and magnificence of a great eagle, but just then a spanking male hen harrier flew right under my nose – then another male and a female, and a short-eared owl not far away. Back to the big one – it now set sail directly for me and came overhead in a long, straight glide. It was a magnificent immature white-tailed eagle – stunning! In 15 minutes it gave just two half-hearted wingbeats. The hugely broad, rounded wings, long head and short tail made its identity obvious even at long range; overhead I could see the spiky tips to all the flight feathers, and its big head swinging from side to side as it surveyed the scene below.

After that, nothing could quite compare – yet the day was far from over. A sparkling flock of 20 choughs, spiralling together in tight formation, kept the excitement going, plus more rock doves and more geese. They were everywhere – another thousand barnacles and 100 white-fronts, before I returned to Gruinart. Golden plovers flickered across the fields, another 16 choughs bounded and bounced about in their inimitable way and 100 shelducks positively glowed in the afternoon light.

For two hours or more I just sat and watched barnacle geese, with the sounds of lapwings, redshanks, oystercatchers, snipe and singing skylarks all around. The next two days were even better for goose numbers – the largest single group of barnacles being 4,000 or so, with a wild, small Canada goose with them, and a brent goose not far away. Peregrines, merlins, many more choughs and black grouse were a most exciting supporting cast. And on the way home, the whole visit was rounded off by the discovery of a fine, adult ring-billed gull!

R.A.H

Field Notes

DATE	TIME
PLACE	

WEATHER CONDITIONS

WIND DIRECTION

NOTES OR SKETCHES

DATE	TIME

PLACE

WEATHER CONDITIONS

WIND DIRECTION

NOTES OR SKETCHES

DATE	TIME

PLACE

WEATHER CONDITIONS

WIND DIRECTION

NOTES OR SKETCHES

Birds From The Cob

Porthmadog. September.

Walking across the Cob gives me a satisfactory feeling of meeting a well-loved friend, and seeing him unchanged. Well, almost unchanged: new buildings have stretched further down towards the road, but the birds are more or less the same. A long expanse of beach is exposed, the sea is only visible in the distance – oystercatchers potter about, kleeping to each other, and a cormorant stands out heraldically, drying its wings. There was another one in the harbour this morning, swimming among the boats. Looking across towards the Moelwyns, beef cattle including some Charolais crosses graze the scrubby, tough plants, along with one or two horses.

The family of swans is still there – five grey cygnets almost as large as their parents. They sail and preen idly in the deeper water near the sluice gates. In the shallow water another family is fishing – red-breasted mergansers, seven of them, all in similar plumage, so if one is the male he must be in eclipse. It's quite a task keeping track of them because one or other is constantly diving. They stay in a small group and patrol the shallows. Suddenly, presumably as they encounter a shoal in a comparatively narrow channel (which must be a good, natural trap for fish), they all dive except one (I speculate that he or she remains a lookout) and then one by one they surface. Sometimes one brings a comparatively large, flattish fish to the surface which it swallows. Then they turn and start to cruise in the other direction.

Much further out, standing motionless, with its neck angled awkwardly, is a heron. It is very grey – one of this year's birds. It looks like an awkward stick, but I have seen it take a stab or two... I can pick out two more herons on the edges of the reeds to the right, and there are probably several others hidden elsewhere. Curlews and redshank call from time to time (their voices carry on into the darkness of the night – it makes an evening walk back from the pub very romantic) and there are several ducks loafing on the banks, but they are a long way out and all in eclipse.

A herring gull is paddling about in a shallow pool – I am enjoying the sharp, clear view of him; his pale, cold, yellow eye, the bright spot of his bill, and pink legs, when he suddenly pounces and pulls out of the soft sandy mud a large crab. The crab is hurled onto the bank; and incredibly it turns to face the gull, aggressively holding out its big front pincers. It doesn't stand a chance – the gull snaps its legs off one by one and then swallows them, attacks the shell, gulps down the body and after a couple more desultory pecks at the now empty carapace, discards it and settles down to preen.

S.M.S

 *Field Notes*

DATE		TIME

PLACE

WEATHER CONDITIONS

WIND DIRECTION

NOTES OR SKETCHES

Date	**Time**

Place

Weather Conditions

Wind Direction

Notes or Sketches

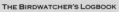

DATE	TIME

PLACE

WIND DIRECTION

NOTES OR SKETCHES

Gannets Off The Mainland

Bempton Cliffs. Mid-April.
The cliffs at Bempton, near Flamborough Head in Humberside, are not the best place to lose a contact lens, especially at the *beginning* of a birdwatching trip. Fortunately, I felt it slip, loosened by the strong wind, and managed to retrieve it, so a potential disaster was averted!

These cliffs are high! I know one reads that they rise 400 feet above the sea, but to actually watch the waves crashing so far below, to see the birds perched precariously on their nesting ledges and to realize that one's own standpoint probably juts out on an overhanging ridge, needs a stronger stomach than mine. I admired those who could casually lean over the guard rails but I felt safer sitting down – at least then I should not be blown off!

The gannets were as good as promised – as spectacular as in the photographs, pristine white with golden necks, hanging in the air against the updraughts on angled wings, and further out to sea, like bright stars against the dark water, shooting down to dive.

The gannets for me were the highlight though many of the party were disappointed not to see the puffins. They were late arriving this year and could only be seen flying past purposefully in small groups, far below and just above the waves. Still, there were the guillemots and razorbills, jackdaws and many, many kittiwakes – always the most attractive of the gulls, with a comparatively mild, benign expression compared with the baleful glare of the herring gulls. The viewing points do give one excellent chances to watch these birds. The fulmars, like the gannets, are effortless in flight – and, watching them on the nesting ledges, I was struck by the mother-of-pearl pink and blueness of their peculiar bill.

Out at sea, those with sharper eyes than mine could pick out rafts of seaducks. Slowly I became more accustomed to watching the rippling water and began to notice some birds bobbing in the valleys of the waves.

A porpoise, rolling quite close to the cliff face, was rather fun, and like anything unexpected, a good bonus.
S.M.S

Field Notes

DATE	TIME

PLACE

WEATHER CONDITIONS

WIND DIRECTION

NOTES OR SKETCHES

DATE	TIME

PLACE

WEATHER CONDITIONS

WIND DIRECTION

NOTES OR SKETCHES

DATE	TIME
PLACE	

WEATHER CONDITIONS

WIND DIRECTION

NOTES OR SKETCHES

Date	Time

Place

Weather Conditions

Wind Direction

Notes or Sketches

Spring At Speyside

Speyside. Mid-May.

Thank goodness the forecast was wrong! We managed to be at Loch Garten reserve at 5.30 am and it was bright, clear and going to be warm. By the gate at the top of Loch Mallachie track we could hear redstart, tree pipit, chaffinch and a great spotted woodpecker. He was drumming so continuously it must have been wearing his beak down. Couldn't see him, but he is certainly not near the birch tree at the top of the track which he used four years ago. That has now been taken over by swifts though they are not back yet. Funny, one never thinks of swifts nesting in trees. Halfway down the track, saw what I assumed was a pair of crested tits, chirring away – cracking wee birds when they are in fine spring plumage, and remarkably tame. They came right down and fed at ground level, while just behind coal tits were doing the same. Just before Loch Mallachie, heard crossbills high up in the pines, but could not see. Their 'chup-chup' call is very distinctive, once you know it.

At Mallachie, singing curlew on the moor on the far side of the loch – very atmospheric. One pair of teal on the loch but little else. Just as I was about to leave realized that there had been continuous bubbling of displaying blackcock from the moor. Must be over a mile away and it's amazing how I missed it. Stared across but couldn't see them. Second species heard but not seen in last five minutes!

Walked the long way back and both heard and saw at least three male capercaillies. They were sitting in some big granny pines, halfway up, and though two of them were crouched quite low on the branch, one was standing in typical displaying pose with its head held high. Further up the path one flew and landed right at the top of the tree, though it didn't make a sound. Lots of tree pipits singing in this open area. The new thinning done last winter is very impressive and I must come back in twenty years to see how it's developing.

Great sitting at the side of Loch Garten having tea and sandwiches at 9 o'clock in the morning before most people are getting ready to go out. Feel as if we have done a full day's birdwatching already. Stared at the loch and hoped to see an osprey, but only common sandpiper and a super male goldeneye which didn't stay long. Cresties calling all over the car while red squirrels crashed about on the other side of the road. First up to the Osprey Observation Point, just to see how things are doing. Everything looked settled and the wardens were looking forward to a warm, comfortable day. Drove round by the back road and managed to see a couple of blackcock on the moor. They were not displaying but were sitting on birch with their tails drooped right down.

Parked at Loch an Eilean and walked to Loch Einich. Longer than I reckoned and didn't get back until after 8 pm, but it was a very pleasant trip. On the first part of the walk through the trees, tree pipit and chaffinch were the

commonest. A superb male redstart was feeding on the track. The main birds, once we had left the trees, were meadow pipits, wheatears and pied wagtails, while when we were nearing Einich we could hear dippers, their song echoing back from the cliffs. Twice saw buzzards, the second was near the Headwalls and should have been an eagle, such was the magnificent setting as it swung round. Hot coming back, though we had to take our boots and shoes off to wade across one of the burns, and that was icy cold.

On the way back, when we were nearing the trees, an osprey flew over. At first glance thought it was a gull but it had that certain something, especially the angled wings, which made us look once more. Wouldn't it be wonderful if they nested once more at Loch an Eilean on the castle! As we were nearing the loch, two red squirrels were so busy chasing each other and getting excited they nearly landed on my head, and even when they saw us they were more interested in each other than ourselves. It must be spring!

F.D.H

Field Notes

DATE	TIME

PLACE

WEATHER CONDITIONS

WIND DIRECTION

NOTES OR SKETCHES

DATE | TIME

PLACE

WEATHER CONDITIONS

WIND DIRECTION

NOTES OR SKETCHES

DATE	TIME
PLACE	

WEATHER CONDITIONS

WIND DIRECTION

NOTES OR SKETCHES

DATE	TIME

PLACE

WEATHER CONDITIONS

WIND DIRECTION

NOTES OR SKETCHES

Flycatchers – A Case Study

These observations of a pied flycatcher were part of a detailed three-year study designed to improve reserve management. The notes are of a male pied flycatcher on The Dinas in Dyfed and were made on 20 April 1982 between 0727 and 0741 hours.

A male pied flycatcher was located and followed. Its position in the wood was determined in relation to a numbered nestbox and its movements recorded while a stopwatch was running continuously. 'Moving up' or 'climbing' refers to gaining height in the tree (height above ground or position in tree given); 'moving uphill' refers to movement from one tree to the next up the slope. Trees are always assumed to be oak, the dominant species, unless stated otherwise. Behaviour and interaction with other birds were also noted.

A key using letters to describe aspects of behaviour, allowed notes to be taken rapidly.

S = singing
C = calling
WF = wing flicking
CA = catching attempt amongst the small branches
CAG = catching attempt on the ground from a perch in the tree
CABR = similar to CAG but attempt made into dead bracken
MIT = moved in the tree, no CA observed

0727   07.27.30. Oak 60yds N of box 56, low branch, CAG, CAG, 10–15yds uphill of box 85, MIT.

0728   3–4ft up, CAG, MIT, MIT, 6ft up, S, MIT, 7ft, CABR, into birch.

0729   4–6ft up, C, oak, C, CAG, uphill to S of box 85.

0730   C, downhill of box 85, S, MIT, C, MIT, mid-canopy, S, MIT, low canopy, S.

0731   Looking down at ground, MIT, looking down, 4ft up, stationary and looking. Occ WF.

0732   MIT, looking down, MIT, looking down, caught insect on trunk, MIT, second bird made CAG nearby.

0733   Second bird CAG, first CAG, moving around, MIT, CAG, second bird within 3ft on low branch, moved to nearby tree, first bird moved to fence.

0734   Second bird CAG, first bird back from fence, second flew off, WF, moving rapidly into mid canopy of tree nr fence, C in flight, C, occ WF.

0735   C, MIT, C, WF, looking up and down, moved up, mid canopy, C, next tree uphill, 20ft up.

0736   S, still climbing, S, CA successful, climbing, C, CA successful, C, S, 35ft up.

0737   S, S, S, 3–4 CA, S, S.

0738   S, S, MIT, in top canopy, S, bill rubbing on branch, S, bill rub, S, bill rub.

0739   Preening.

0740   S, preening, S, preening, S, S, CA, top canopy, S, S.

0741   Moved down, S, lost 07.41.16.

T.S

Field Notes

DATE	**TIME**
PLACE	

WEATHER CONDITIONS

WIND DIRECTION

NOTES OR SKETCHES

DATE	TIME
PLACE	

WEATHER CONDITIONS

WIND DIRECTION

NOTES OR SKETCHES

DATE	TIME

PLACE

WEATHER CONDITIONS

WIND DIRECTION

NOTES OR SKETCHES

DATE	TIME

PLACE

WEATHER CONDITIONS

WIND DIRECTION

NOTES OR SKETCHES

Rare Birds

'On July 31st 1952, one of us was given a description of a strange pigeon or dove that had been seen in and around the grounds of a hall in the parish of Manton, north Lincolnshire.' That report, by Reg May and James Fisher, published in the monthly journal *British Birds,* was the first British record of the collared dove. Over the next few years birdwatchers vied with each other to add the collared dove to their British list, but now it is one of our commonest birds – so much so that it can even be an agricultural pest!

So what is a rare bird? The question sounds deceptively simple, but the definition can vary endlessly according to geographical location, habitat and circumstances. To the birdwatcher in Scotland a nuthatch is a rare bird; to someone in central and southern England wild geese are unusual, while birdwatchers in Ireland would have to come to England to hear tawny owls and woodpeckers. A heron beside the riverbank may cause little comment: if one turns up to raid your garden pond, it is more likely to provoke a reaction. Blackcaps are widespread summer migrants, but when these little warblers first began to visit birdtables in winter, birdwatchers studied their habits with renewed interest.

Because Great Britain is on the extreme west of Europe, many birds are on the periphery of their geographical range and only occur in small numbers here, but on a world basis their populations are healthy and just a short journey across the English Channel they can be easily seen. More bird species breed in this country now than at the turn of the century and the British List continues to grow. Some birds are recorded each year with increasing frequency, sometimes possibly due to changing weather trends, but more probably because of the growing popularity of birdwatching and the improving standards of identification.

So where do you go if you want to see rare birds? For vagrants and accidentals – unusual migrants that have strayed beyond their normal range – a visit to a bird observatory, especially in spring and autumn, can be very rewarding. At opposite ends of Great Britain, Fair Isle in the north-east and the Isles of Scilly at the south-westerly tip regularly attract large numbers of birdwatchers all hopeful of seeing another 'lifer'.

Rare breeding birds should generally be left well alone. (Those on Schedule I of the Wildlife and Countryside Act are given extra protection and intentional disturbance can result in a heavy fine.) Some are exceptionally vulnerable to disturbance when nesting. Even if the adults do not appear to be distressed, your presence could cause them to slip off the nest for a few minutes, exposing precious eggs or young chicks to marauding predators. Fortunately, many rarities, including ospreys, little terns and avocets, marsh harriers and bitterns, can be seen easily on reserves from the safe distance of a hide. Recently the RSPB also introduced a special public viewing scheme for peregrines at Symonds Yat Rock, a noted beauty spot in Gloucestershire. If you find a rare breeding bird, the best policy is to keep it absolutely secret, unless you feel it is in need of protection, in which case inform the RSPB.

It is the cherished ambition of many birdwatchers to have one of their own records accepted by the Rarities Committee. This committee consists of ten of the country's top ornithologists, who examine all the reports submitted to them. Each year, those accepted are printed in the Report on Rare Birds in Great Britain, published in the monthly journal *British Birds*.

Even if you do not have a bird that qualifies as a rarity on a national scale, you may well see one that is unusual for your county, which brings us back to the original question. A county rarity should be reported to your county bird recorder, while a list of the species considered by the Rarities Committee can be obtained from the honorary secretary. In any case you will need to submit a full description of the bird (plus details of place, habitat, weather conditions and date) based on your actual field notes. This is another good reason for taking accurate field notes, because one day you too might see a first for Britain!

Field Notes

DATE	TIME

PLACE

WEATHER CONDITIONS

WIND DIRECTION

NOTES OR SKETCHES

DATE	TIME

PLACE

WEATHER CONDITIONS

WIND DIRECTION

NOTES OR SKETCHES

DATE	TIME

PLACE

WEATHER CONDITIONS

WIND DIRECTION

NOTES OR SKETCHES

A Special Swift

Berry Head, Devon. 18 August 1985.
Weather: 6/8 cloud cover; westerly winds force 4–5; Low cloud, occasional rain.

Told that an alpine swift had roosted in the limestone quarry at Berry Head for eight nights, I visited the site on a cool dull evening.

Arriving at 6.15 pm, I hoped to watch the bird in good light before it went to roost. On previous evenings the alpine swift had hawked the cliff top from approximately 6.30 pm. Walking through the fort gates that once defended the headland, I was surprised to see 100 – 150 birdwatchers! The restored battlements actually assisted this invasion, providing vantage points. This long-staying bird offered an excellent chance for many birdwatchers to catch up with this notorious 'one-day' species.

6.35 pm: four arctic skuas passed the headland; one pale phase and one dark phase adult, followed by two dark juveniles.

The next hour produced little more than idle gossip, cups of coffee and crooked necks, as every distant herring gull and starling was scrutinized. The light had started to go. Now everyone doubted the swift's return.

'There it is!' At 7.40 pm the alpine swift soared lazily over our heads, showing its characteristic pale belly patch before banking into a steep falcon-like descent. A low murmur of appreciation passed through the crowd, as the bird veered around an outcrop. The next minute seemed like ten. I feared the cold August evening had sent the swift to roost early. Then, like magic, the alpine swift reappeared, gliding over our heads. Teasing the spectators, the bird must have flown the full circuit of Berry Head. Staying high, scything through the low cloud, it gave a good chance to take a description.

Size: with nothing but herring gulls for comparison, the swift did not appear as large as I expected. The body however was quite stocky.

Wings: not as pointed as common swift. Upper and lower wings were brown, looking very dark in the dull light.

Upperparts: brown from head to tail. Tail and wings slightly darker than the rest of the body. Large, dark inset eye gave a masked appearance.

Underparts: large pale belly patch from breast to vent. Tail and under tail coverts dark brown. The throat patch was indistinct (perhaps a first-year bird). A dark breast band divided off the front third of the bird.

Binoculars were not needed as the swift hawked at cliff-top level less than 20 feet away. Despite the cold and damp, it quartered Berry Head for 22 minutes before finally diving into a crevice on the quarry face.

A.M.L

Elusive Birds

Some birds are elusive by nature and others always seem to evade you, as if it was something personal. The bird in question may not be rare, or even particularly exciting, but somehow you just can't get to see it.

As well as that kind of elusive bird, most birdwatchers have a private list of special birds they would really like to see one day. Some birds qualify here simply because they fire the imagination – birds such as golden eagles, skimmers, bee-eaters and vultures. They represent travel, adventure, the fulfilment of dreams.

In the pages that follow we have left space for six species of dream bird and/or awkward bird. See how many you can fill. To encourage you never to give up trying, we print below the story of one birdwatcher's long-awaited success.

The Jynx

Most birdwatchers have their bogey bird. Mine was the wryneck. From the day I opened my first bird book I had wanted to see this species more than any other but always I had been unlucky.

To make things more difficult, I'm not in the habit of tuning in to the 'grapevine' and dashing off to hotspots in the migration season. I would rather work my own unfashionable patch of Sussex downland and wait (and wait…) for the birds to come to me. If my 'rarities' are redstarts rather than bluethroats, well at least I've found them for myself.

Having a nightshift job can be a mixed blessing to a birdwatcher and ringer, especially in the autumn: it is so tempting to try and burn the candle at both ends. Weather conditions one Monday in early September were too good to resist. A clear sky and light easterly winds had me striding for miles over the downs checking out those stunted, straggly hawthorn hedges that the redstarts like, instead of resting quietly in preparation for the hard night's work ahead.

And at last there was a redstart, as I knew there would be, flickering and dodging and flycatching its way from bush to bush, showing off that glorious tail. Catching and ringing it took much longer than I had allowed for, and it was a mad rush to get back to the farm, feed the horses, cycle home, even feed myself! – and arrive at work on time to start the $10\frac{1}{2}$-hour shift. It had been a splendid day, but I would suffer for it later, in that dead hour of four in the morning when all biorhythms are at their lowest ebb.

The dawn brought new strength, but I was still in no condition to appreciate the pleasant one-mile walk home through downland fields. At last I stood before my own front door, thinking only of a cup of tea and a welcome bed. Then slowly the realization penetrated my fuddled brain. I had forgotten my key. It was in my locker at work. I would have to go back. Like a zombie I turned and shambled off up the hill.

Behind the factories are car parks below a derelict hillside crossed by a paved footpath. Plodding down the concrete steps, I cursed my luck, and the minor loss of face to come. How my mates (still working overtime) would laugh when I came sneaking back in. What rotten, wretched luck! Why did I have to forget my key, today of all days? It was several seconds before my subconscious mind could break through this shell of self-pity to tell me there was something very odd about the bird on the path in front of me, a bird of a dozen different shades of fawn and brown, a bird now shuffling like a dunnock, now perching jerkily on the handrails like a woodpecker, now twisting its head and displaying that peculiar black mark on its nape...

I could almost reach out and touch it... It was a wryneck.

R.L

Elusive Birds

SPECIES	DATE	PLACE

COMMENTS

SPECIES	DATE	PLACE

COMMENTS

SPECIES	DATE	PLACE

COMMENTS

SPECIES	DATE	PLACE

COMMENTS

SPECIES	DATE	PLACE

COMMENTS

SPECIES	DATE	PLACE

COMMENTS

THE BIRDWATCHER'S LOGBOOK

Holiday Plans

Plan your birdwatching holiday with care. If you have only yourself to think about, it is usually less of a problem, but if you are accompanied by a spouse and children who may not be quite as enthusiastic as you are, then you will want to choose a holiday that can cater for their interests too.

Don't expect everyone to be content to spend each and every day staring out to sea from dawn to dusk, or tramping for hours across mile upon mile of damp and misty Scottish moorland in the faint hope of glimpsing a golden eagle. Get up early – it's much the best time to see birds anyway – and enjoy a couple of hours' solitary birdwatching, before reconciling yourself to keeping half an eye on the children while they make sandcastles on the beach.

All children have a low boredom threshold, so keep your birdwatching trips with them short, and maintain their curiosity by pointing out other items of interest, and by playing games. Play 'Red Indians' on the beach and try to read the many tracks and signs left in the sand. Who can be the first to identify 10 different plants? Try stalking a singing bird until you can see it. On car journeys get the children to look for pub signs with pictures of birds and bird names. It's worth 'spoon-feeding' those whose interest in birds needs to be nurtured: few people could fail to be enthralled by the ospreys at Loch Garten or the delicate avocets at Minsmere, but non-birdwatchers do tend to be unimpressed by trips to see birds which do not oblige on the day!

Questions to ask yourself when planning your holiday will basically be the same whether you intend to go abroad or stay nearer to home. Which area should you choose? Are you going touring or will you be based at one particular spot? Do you want to see certain species? If so, what is the best time of year and where is the best place to go? How about a birdwatching course?

Courses and organized tours can provide pleasant companionship with like-minded people as well as useful instruction from expert ornithologists and naturalists. Some travel firms are able to offer courses especially tailored to meet individual requirements, while others may combine another interest such as botany or painting. If you have children who have reached an age where they would revel in a holiday separate from mum and dad, the Young Ornithologists' Club also organizes short residential courses.

Having decided where you want to go, buy one or two Ordnance Survey maps of the area, read about the local habitats and birdlife (most county bird clubs publish an annual report – the address of the secretary should be available from your public library). There are also many books on the birdlife of particular regions and the best places for birdwatching. One that has become almost a standard is John Gooders's *Where to Watch Birds* (Pan).

If you are going abroad, the same principles apply. Organized tours are obviously the most expensive, but generally offer excellent accommodation and enable you to avoid the delays and pitfalls that can so easily befall the lone traveller. Brochures usually have detailed information on the birds you can hope to see, accommodation, transport, the maximum number of the party, and a short biography of the leader. The firm should give a reading list and other advice on customs, climate and clothing, visa and vaccination requirements.

Those with a greater sense of adventure, who enjoy planning their own itineraries, map-reading, and do not mind roughing it if necessary, may prefer to make their own arrangements. Birdwatchers with young children can get excellent value from a package holiday to one of the popular resorts. The hotels and immediate surroundings usually offer ample amusement for children and sun-worshippers, while exotic birds can be seen from the terraces and balconies, and a short excursion soon leads you away from the crowds and into more remote countryside. If you are able to take advantage of end-of-season prices, the spring and autumn often offer more interesting and spectacular birdwatching.

Apart from obtaining the necessary vaccinations, remember that in some areas insects can be troublesome, so do take a supply of insect-repellent cream or lotion. If you are travelling outside Europe, anti-malaria tablets are a very wise precaution – check with your doctor. Also, do steer clear of military zones, unless you welcome a brush with the authorities. Birdwatchers' camouflaged jackets, binoculars and cameras are bound to arouse suspicion, and even if you are fluent in the language of the country a run-in with the military police is at best unnerving and at worst could land you in a foreign gaol. It is certainly not unknown for people caught in such circumstances to have the film in their camera destroyed.

Most European countries have their own conservation and birdwatching organizations. They nearly all operate on a shoestring budget and few of them have the nationwide network of reserves to be found in Great Britain and the United States, so they need all the support they can get. For more information about them, contact the International Council for Bird Preservation.

If you need guidance on where to go, try to find a copy of John Gooders's book, *Where to Watch Birds in Europe.* In addition, the RSPB produces birdwatching information leaflets on several countries. And if you cannot decide on the type of holiday you would like, have a browse through the RSPB's quarterly magazine, *Birds.* From cruises, courses, camping, self-catering cottages, luxury hotels to wildlife tours and safaris, you will find something to meet all tastes. As with anything else, a little advance planning can save a lot of time and possible disappointment. So make your birdwatching holiday memorable for its good days rather than its disasters!

The Birdwatcher's Library

All birdwatchers are collectors at heart; they 'collect' birds, so why not collect birdbooks too? The wealth of birdbooks in the shops today is ample evidence of the enormous interest in the subject. There are field guides, area guides, guides on where to watch birds, handbooks, monographs, books of photographs, paintings and poetry – the list is almost endless. The experienced birder will soon be able to decide which books he personally finds useful, but the newcomer to birdwatching could be bewildered.

If you have not already done so, invest in at least one good field guide. There are several excellent ones on the market which are now regarded as standard works and each devotee will swear by his own particular favourite. In addition, as standards of identification have improved, a number of more specialized books have emerged on particular groups of birds, such as waders, wildfowl, birds of prey and seabirds. If you have yet to buy a guide to bird identification, examine some of the following to see which will suit you best:

Heinzel, Fitter and Parslow, *The Birds of Britain and Europe* (Collins).

Bruun and Singer, *The Hamlyn Guide to Birds of Britain and Europe* (Hamlyn).

Peterson, Mountfort and Hollom, *A Field Guide to the Birds of Britain and Europe* (Collins).

Saunders, *The RSPB Guide to British Birds* (Hamlyn).

Ferguson-Lees, Willis and Sharrock, *The Shell Guide to the Birds of Britain and Ireland* (Michael Joseph).

Hume, *Birds of Britain and Europe* (Usborne).

Hayman, *The Birdlife of Britain* (Mitchell Beazley).

Hayman, *The Mitchell Beazley Birdwatchers Pocket Guide* (Mitchell Beazley).

Hayman and Everett, *What's that Bird?* (RSPB).

You will also need a handbook which gives information about birds' lifestyles and habits. Try a short reference book such as *The Popular Handbook of British Birds* by P.A.D. Hollom (Witherby) which contains a great deal of information, or the excellent little *RSPB Book of British Birds* by Peter Holden and Tim Sharrock (Macmillan). You may be lucky enough to have the five volumes of Witherby's *Handbook of British Birds,* but most serious birders today are collecting the seven volumes of the most up-to-date, definitive work, *The Handbook of the Birds of Europe, the Middle East and North Africa* (often referred to as BWP – Birds of the Western Palearctic), which is published by Oxford University Press.

With a good field guide and a general handbook, you will have a sound basis on which to start birdwatching. For a superb introduction to the hobby, especially with regard to fieldcraft, try *The RSPB Guide to Birdwatching* by Peter Conder (Hamlyn), or, for children, *The Young Birdwatcher* by Nicholas Hammond (Hamlyn).

The Atlas of Breeding Birds of Britain and Ireland by Tim Sharrock (Poyser) will give you an idea of the breeding distribution of birds, and has inspired several county bird clubs to produce similar books containing a more detailed breakdown of distribution in their area. A book about the birdlife of your own county or region might be very useful, while for birdwatching on a national scale, apart from John Gooders's *Where to Watch Birds* (Pan), you may like to look at *RSPB Nature Reserves* edited by Nicholas Hammond (RSPB) or the *Guide to Britain's Nature Reserves* (Macmillan).

Another reference book worth considering is *The Birdwatcher's Yearbook,* which contains all sorts of useful material, and just about any address a birdwatcher could need. After building up a reasonable library, you may wish to specialize: some people collect books on bird art or photographs, others concentrate on a particular bird species or group. Still others make a practice of collecting all the publications in a series such as Collins New Naturalist, or they particularly enjoy birdwatching diaries or biographies.

Apart from RSPB shops (which carry stocks of many popular titles), the other specialist place to buy your books is The Bird Bookshop, in Edinburgh, which also has an excellent mail-order service. If you don't have a birdwatcher's library, now is the time to start! Once you have started, keep a record of your acquisitions on the following pages.

The Birdwatcher's Library

AUTHOR & TITLE	REMARKS

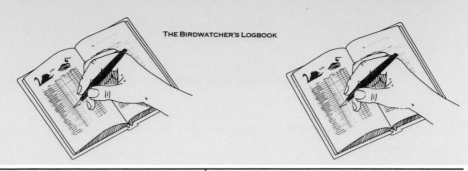

AUTHOR & TITLE	REMARKS

Lend A Hand!

Clearing scrub, felling trees, painting signposts, mending walls and fences, making nestboxes, chatting to visitors, searching for errant lambs, or chasing potential nest-robbers – a voluntary warden's life is often hard work, but it's never dull. Perhaps this is why so many people give up a week or more of their annual holidays to help warden a reserve or man an information centre. Others take part in the protection schemes to keep a vigilant eye on isolated rare breeding birds.

Most conservation organizations rely heavily on voluntary support and the simplest action any birdwatcher can take to ensure the future of his hobby is to join the RSPB. Apart from the benefits he receives directly, such as free access to reserves, his subscription plays a vital part in helping to protect birds and other wildlife. Don't make the mistake of thinking that most of your subscription is swallowed up in administrative costs – of the current £12 RSPB subscription, only £3.00 goes on 'servicing', including sending the Society's magazine, *Birds*. The remainder is spent directly on other work such as managing reserves, research, organizing special protection schemes, education and making films. Remember, too, that the more members a conservation organization has, the more powerfully it can argue its case when fighting threats to wildlife and habitat.

If rhododendron-bashing is simply not for you, don't despair: there are countless other ways for you to make an active contribution. From keeping records, organizing fund-raising activities, addressing envelopes or making cakes, there really is something for everyone, no matter what your age. So join your local RSPB members' group or your county naturalists' trust. If you like children, why not become a YOC leader? Get to know the warden of your nearest reserve and see what you can do to help. If you do not have a garden of your own or need something extra to get your teeth into, talk to a churchwarden or parish councillor to see what improvements could be made for wildlife to your churchyard or recreation ground, for instance the planting of a few berry-bearing shrubs or leaving a patch of grass unmown.

Opposite is a page on which you can record all your good deeds, so don't wait to be asked!

ORGANIZATION

DATE | PLACE

TASK UNDERTAKEN

COMMENTS

ORGANIZATION

DATE | PLACE

TASK UNDERTAKEN

COMMENTS

ORGANIZATION

DATE | PLACE

TASK UNDERTAKEN

COMMENTS

ORGANIZATION

DATE | PLACE

TASK UNDERTAKEN

COMMENTS

Lists For Birdwatchers

At New Year many birdwatchers resolve to add to their life-list and to see more birds this year than last. Some take this so seriously that they make a New Year's Day 'tick-hunt' a regular event to ensure they get off to a good start. Birdwatchers are compulsive list-keepers and while most will have a 'life-list' and a 'year-list', and very probably a 'holiday-list', others will go to extraordinary lengths. A British list, plus separate lists for the garden, county, local patch and even the month – these are quite common, but some birdwatchers keep lists of birds they have seen on television and even those they have dreamt about!

There are about 510 bird species on the British and Irish List compiled by the British Ornithologists' Union and the Irish Wildbird Conservancy, although only about half of these are regularly seen. This list includes breeding and wintering birds, regular passage migrants, vagrants and those which have either been introduced or have escaped from captivity and established a feral population. Worldwide there are some 8,600 species, which would keep you occupied for quite some time. According to the American Birding Association, a gentleman called Norman Chesterfield has seen the most birds, with more than 6,000 species on his list.

Incidentally, as with any other game, there are a few generally accepted rules. For a species to 'count' it must be a genuine wild bird. Exotic specimens which have just escaped from an aviary or collection are not, strictly speaking, eligible. Nor are those tired migrants which have hitched a lift on a ship, or those which have been washed up on shore, or found dead inland. Some purists are even unhappy about long-established but introduced birds such as pheasant and red-legged partridge!

List-making creates an atmosphere of competitiveness in a pastime that is essentially uncompetitive. No doubt it fulfils the human need for a challenge, as the continuing popularity of the RSPB's annual sponsored birdwatch shows. For several years, two expert teams have competed against each other in an attempt to capture the record for the largest number of species seen in a day. Helped by fast cars, helicopters and aeroplanes, they start at dawn and do not finish until midnight. Through sponsorship they have raised several thousand pounds for wildlife charities, and their current record is 151 species in the course of the day – so now you know what you have to aim for!

Your Own Lists

Use these pages to record your life-list, and in the right-hand columns keep a count of the species you see in the course of three separate years. These lists are followed by three holiday-lists.

      The named birds have been limited to British birds (and by no means every species on the British List has been included) and there are extra lines for you to add European species and any other birds you happen to see. The birds are listed in the scientific order used in most bird books, and symbols have been added to indicate when they are most likely to be seen.

Key to Symbols

R = resident – species present throughout year
S = summer visitor – breeds here
W = winter visitor
M = migrant – occurs on passage

Life-list

	SPECIES	STATUS	FIRST SEEN		YEAR LIST		
			DATE	PLACE	19	19	19
DIVERS	RED-THROATED DIVER	R					
	BLACK-THROATED DIVER	R					
	GREAT NORTHERN DIVER	W					
GREBES	LITTLE GREBE	R					
	GREAT CRESTED GREBE	R					
	RED-NECKED GREBE	W					
	SLAVONIAN GREBE	W					
	BLACK-NECKED GREBE	MW					
TUBENOSES	FULMAR	S					
	GREAT SHEARWATER	M					
	MANX SHEARWATER	S					
	SOOTY SHEARWATER	M					
	STORM PETREL	S					
	LEACH'S PETREL	S					
	GANNET	S					
	CORMORANT	R					
	SHAG	R					
HERONS	BITTERN	R					
	GREY HERON	R					
	SPOONBILL	M					
SWANS	MUTE SWAN	R					
	BEWICK'S SWAN	W					
	WHOOPER SWAN	W					
GEESE	BEAN GOOSE	W					
	PINK-FOOTED GOOSE	W					
	WHITE-FRONTED GOOSE	W					

	Species	Status	First Seen		Year List		
			Date	Place	19	19	19
GEESE AND DUCKS	GREYLAG GOOSE	W					
	CANADA GOOSE	R					
	BARNACLE GOOSE	W					
	BRENT GOOSE	W					
	EGYPTIAN GOOSE	R					
	SHELDUCK	R					
	MANDARIN	R					
	WIGEON	W					
	GADWALL	RW					
	TEAL	RW					
	MALLARD	R					
	PINTAIL	W					
	GARGANEY	S					
	SHOVELER	RW					
	RED-CRESTED POCHARD	W					
	POCHARD	W					
	TUFTED DUCK	RW					
	SCAUP	W					
	EIDER	R					
	LONG-TAILED DUCK	W					
	COMMON SCOTER	MW					
	VELVET SCOTER	W					
	GOLDENEYE	W					
	SMEW	W					
	RED-BREASTED MERGANSER	RW					
	GOOSANDER	W					

| | SPECIES | STATUS | FIRST SEEN | | YEAR LIST | | |
			DATE	PLACE	19	19	19
	RUDDY DUCK	R					
BIRDS OF PREY	HONEY BUZZARD	S					
	RED KITE	R					
	WHITE-TAILED EAGLE	R					
	MARSH HARRIER	SR					
	HEN HARRIER	RW					
	MONTAGU'S HARRIER	S					
	GOSHAWK	R					
	SPARROWHAWK	R					
	BUZZARD	R					
	ROUGH-LEGGED BUZZARD	W					
	GOLDEN EAGLE	R					
	OSPREY	S M					
	KESTREL	R					
	MERLIN	R					
	HOBBY	S					
	PEREGRINE	R					
GAME BIRDS	RED GROUSE	R					
	PTARMIGAN	R					
	BLACK GROUSE	R					
	CAPERCAILLIE	R					
	RED-LEGGED PARTRIDGE	R					
	GREY PARTRIDGE	R					
	QUAIL	S					
	PHEASANT	R					
	GOLDEN PHEASANT	R					

	Species	Status	First Seen		Year Lis		
			Date	Place	19	19	19
	Lady Amherst's Pheasant	R					
Crakes & Rails	Water Rail	RW					
	Spotted Crake	SM					
	Corncrake	S					
	Moorhen	RW					
	Coot	RW					
Waders	Oystercatcher	RW					
	Avocet	S					
	Stone Curlew	S					
	Little Ringed Plover	S					
	Ringed Plover	RMW					
	Kentish Plover	M					
	Dotterel	SM					
	Golden Plover	RMW					
	Grey Plover	MW					
	Lapwing	R					
	Knot	MW					
	Sanderling	MW					
	Little Stint	M					
	Temminck's Stint	M					
	Pectoral Sandpiper	M					
	Curlew Sandpiper	M					
	Purple Sandpiper	MW					
	Dunlin	MW					
	Ruff	M					
	Jack Snipe	MW					

	SPECIES	STATUS	FIRST SEEN		YEAR LIST		
			DATE	PLACE	19	19	19
WADERS	SNIPE	R					
	WOODCOCK	RW					
	BLACK-TAILED GODWIT	MW					
	BAR-TAILED GODWIT	MW					
	WHIMBREL	M					
	CURLEW	R					
	SPOTTED REDSHANK	M					
	REDSHANK	R					
	GREENSHANK	M					
	GREEN SANDPIPER	M					
	WOOD SANDPIPER	M					
	COMMON SANDPIPER	SW					
	TURNSTONE	MW					
	RED-NECKED PHALAROPE	S					
	GREY PHALAROPE	M					
SKUAS	POMARINE SKUA	M					
	ARCTIC SKUA	S					
	GREAT SKUA	S					
GULLS	MEDITERRANEAN GULL	M					
	LITTLE GULL	M					
	COMMON GULL	R					
	BLACK-HEADED GULL	RW					
	LESSER BLACK-BACKED GULL	S					
	HERRING GULL	RW					
	ICELAND GULL	W					
	GLAUCOUS GULL	W					

SPECIES	STATUS	FIRST SEEN		YEAR LIST		
		DATE	PLACE	19	19	19
GREAT BLACK-BACKED GULL	RW					
KITTIWAKE	RS					
TERNS SANDWICH TERN	S					
ROSEATE TERN	S					
COMMON TERN	S					
ARCTIC TERN	S					
LITTLE TERN	S					
BLACK TERN	M					
AUKS GUILLEMOT	R					
RAZORBILL	R					
BLACK GUILLEMOT	R					
LITTLE AUK	W					
PUFFIN	S					
PIGEONS & DOVES ROCK DOVE	R					
STOCK DOVE	R					
WOOD PIGEON	R					
COLLARED DOVE	R					
TURTLE DOVE	S					
RING-NECKED PARAKEET	R					
CUCKOO	S					
OWLS BARN OWL	R					
LITTLE OWL	R					
TAWNY OWL	R					
LONG-EARED OWL	R					
SHORT-EARED OWL	RW					
NIGHTJAR	S					

	SPECIES	STATUS	FIRST SEEN		YEAR LIST		
			DATE	PLACE	19	19	19
	SWIFT	S					
	KINGFISHER	R					
	HOOPOE	M					
WOODPECKERS	WRYNECK	M					
WOODPECKERS	GREEN WOODPECKER	R					
WOODPECKERS	GREAT SPOTTED WOODPECKER	R					
WOODPECKERS	LESSER SPOTTED WOODPECKER	R					
LARKS	WOODLARK	R					
LARKS	SKYLARK	RW					
LARKS	SHORE LARK	W					
SWALLOWS & MARTINS	SAND MARTIN	S					
SWALLOWS & MARTINS	SWALLOW	S					
SWALLOWS & MARTINS	HOUSE MARTIN	S					
PIPITS & WAGTAILS	TREE PIPIT	S					
PIPITS & WAGTAILS	MEADOW PIPIT	SMW					
PIPITS & WAGTAILS	ROCK PIPIT	R					
PIPITS & WAGTAILS	YELLOW WAGTAIL	S					
PIPITS & WAGTAILS	GREY WAGTAIL	R					
PIPITS & WAGTAILS	PIED WAGTAIL	R					
	WAXWING	W					
	DIPPER	R					
	WREN	R					
	DUNNOCK	R					
CHATS	ROBIN	R					
CHATS	NIGHTINGALE	S					
CHATS	BLUETHROAT	M					

| | SPECIES | STATUS | FIRST SEEN | | YEAR LIST | | |
			DATE	PLACE	19	19	19
CHATS	BLACK REDSTART	SM					
	REDSTART	S					
	WHINCHAT	S					
	STONECHAT	R					
	WHEATEAR	SM					
THRUSHES	RING OUZEL	S					
	BLACKBIRD	R					
	FIELDFARE	MW					
	SONG THRUSH	R					
	REDWING	MW					
	MISTLE THRUSH	R					
WARBLERS	CETTI'S WARBLER	R					
	GRASSHOPPER WARBLER	S					
	SAVI'S WARBLER	S					
	SEDGE WARBLER	S					
	MARSH WARBLER	S					
	REED WARBLER	S					
	DARTFORD WARBLER	R					
	LESSER WHITETHROAT	S					
	WHITETHROAT	S					
	GARDEN WARBLER	S					
	BLACKCAP	S					
	WOOD WARBLER	S					
	CHIFFCHAFF	S					
	WILLOW WARBLER	S					
	GOLDCREST	RMW					

| | SPECIES | STATUS | FIRST SEEN | | YEAR LIST | | |
			DATE	PLACE	19	19	19
	FIRECREST	M					
	SPOTTED FLYCATCHER	S					
	PIED FLYCATCHER	SM					
TITS	BEARDED TIT	R					
	LONG-TAILED TIT	R					
	MARSH TIT	R					
	WILLOW TIT	R					
	CRESTED TIT	R					
	COAL TIT	R					
	BLUE TIT	R					
	GREAT TIT	R					
	NUTHATCH	R					
	TREECREEPER	R					
	GOLDEN ORIOLE	M					
SHRIKES	RED-BACKED SHRIKE	SM					
	GREAT GREY SHRIKE	W					
CROWS	JAY	R					
	MAGPIE	R					
	CHOUGH	R					
	JACKDAW	R					
	ROOK	R					
	CARRION CROW/HOODED CROW	R					
	RAVEN	R					
	STARLING	R					
	HOUSE SPARROW	R					
	TREE SPARROW	R					

| | SPECIES | STATUS | FIRST SEEN | | YEAR LIST | | |
			DATE	PLACE	19	19	19
BUNTINGS	LAPLAND BUNTING	M					
	SNOW BUNTING	W					
	YELLOWHAMMER	R					
	CIRL BUNTING	R					
	REED BUNTING	R					
	CORN BUNTING	R					
FINCHES	CHAFFINCH	R					
	BRAMBLING	W					
	SERIN	S					
	GREENFINCH	R					
	GOLDFINCH	R					
	SISKIN	R					
	LINNET	R					
	TWITE	R					
	REDPOLL	R					
	CROSSBILL	RW					
	SCOTTISH CROSSBILL	R					
	BULLFINCH	R					
	HAWFINCH	R					

| | SPECIES | STATUS | FIRST SEEN | | YEAR LIST | | |
			DATE	PLACE	19	19	19

Holiday Lists

PLACE	DATE
ITINERARY	

WEATHER CONDITIONS

COMMENTS

SPECIES	

THE BIRDWATCHER'S LOGBOOK

PLACE	DATE

ITINERARY

WEATHER CONDITIONS

COMMENTS

SPECIES	

PLACE	DATE

ITINERARY

WEATHER CONDITIONS

COMMENTS

SPECIES	

The Birdwatcher's Directory

These selective lists contain the names and addresses of organizations and suppliers of particular interest to birdwatchers. For local addresses such as your county bird club, bird recorder or RSPB members' group, consult *The Birdwatcher's Yearbook,* the RSPB or your public library.

Societies

Royal Society for the Protection of Birds, The Lodge, Sandy, Bedfordshire SG19 2DL; 0767 80551.

Founded in 1889, the RSPB is Europe's largest wildlife conservation organization, with a membership of over 400,000. It manages over 100 reserves, covering more than 100,000 acres. Its activities include investigating offences under the bird protection laws, research into threats affecting birds, monitoring of pollution, special protection schemes, conservation planning, international liaison and education. It has a nationwide network of local members' groups and publishes a quarterly magazine, *Birds,* which is sent to all members. The Society's mail-order sales department and shops stock many items including binoculars, books and garden bird equipment.

RSPB regional offices:

Scotland: 17 Regent Terrace, Edinburgh EH7 5BN; 031-556 5624.

Northern Ireland: Belvoir Park Forest, Belfast BT8 4QT; 0232 69547.

Wales: Frolic Street, Newtown, Powys SY16 2NP; 0686 26678.

East Anglia: Aldwych House, Bethel Street, Norwich NR2 1NR; 0603 615920.

East Midlands: 12 Guildhall Street, Lincoln LN1 1TT; 0522 35596.

Midlands: 44 Friar Street, Droitwich, Worcestershire WR9 8ED; 0905 770581.

North of England: 'E' Floor, Milburn House, Dean Street, Newcastle upon Tyne NE1 1LE; 0632 324148.

North-west England: Imperial House, Imperial Arcade, Huddersfield, West Yorkshire HD1 2BR; 0484 36331.

South-east England: Scan House, 4 Church Street, Shoreham-by-Sea, West Sussex BN4 5DQ; 079-17 63642.

South-west England: 10 Richmond Road, Exeter, Devon EX4 4JA; 0392 32691.

Young Ornithologists' Club (YOC), The Lodge, Sandy, Bedfordshire SG19 2DL; 0767 80551.

The junior section of the RSPB, the YOC has about 85,000 members, who receive its magazine *Bird Life,* published six times a year, and can partake in national surveys and projects and competitions. The YOC also organizes holiday courses and has more than 400 local members' groups throughout the country.

British Ornithologists' Union, c/o Zoological Society of London, Regents Park, London NW1 4RY.
Members of the BOU include some of the most respected ornithologists in the world. The BOU publishes a quarterly journal, *The Ibis*.

British Trust for Ornithology, Beech Grove, Tring, Herts HP23 5NR; 044282 3461.
Formed in 1933, the BTO is financed by membership subscriptions (current 8,000) and contracts from the Nature Conservancy Council. Its aim is the study of bird populations, their distribution, numbers and movements, and of the ecological factors, including those of human origin, affecting them. It maintains a staff of trained biologists at Tring who collaborate with a network of amateur birdwatchers throughout the country, taking part in a wide-ranging programme of surveys and bird ringing. It communicates the results of these co-operative efforts to government departments, local authorities and conservation bodies for effective action. It awards grants, gives guidance to and helps members in their own research, holds national and regional conferences, runs specialist courses and publishes two journals and a two-monthly news bulletin.

International Council for Bird Preservation, Hon Sec R.D. Chancellor, c/o Institute of Biology, 20 Queensbury Place, London SW7 2DZ. Headquarters: 219c Huntingdon Road, Cambridge; 0223 277318.
The ICBP was the first international conservation body to be set up, over sixty years ago. It is the chief adviser to the International Union for the Conservation of Nature (IUCN) on all bird conservation problems, it promotes research projects and protection measures for endangered and vulnerable bird species, and co-ordinates the work of national bird protection societies with national sections or representatives in 75 different countries.

Irish Wildbird Conservancy, Southview, Church Road, Greystones, Co Wicklow; Dublin (01) 875759.
The IWC is a national voluntary organization for the conservation of wild birds and their habitats. Research and education are among its main activities and it also manages a number of reserves. The journal *Irish Birds* is published by the IWC.

Royal Society for Nature Conservation, The Green, Nettleham, Lincoln LN2 2NR; 0522 752326.
The RSNC is the national association of the Nature Conservation Trusts. The RSNC advises and gives assistance to the Trusts on a wide range of matters related to nature conservation. Between them the Trusts and the RSNC own or manage

some 1,600 nature reserves, covering nearly 115,000 acres. The Society has a club for young people, called WATCH which is co-sponsored by the Sunday Times, and publishes a magazine, *Natural World,* three times a year.

Scottish Ornithologists' Club, 21 Regent Terrace, Edinburgh EH7 5BT.
The SOC was founded in 1936 and now has nearly 3,000 members and 13 branches throughout Scotland. The SOC publishes a twice-yearly journal *Scottish Birds* incorporating the annual *Scottish Bird Report* and a quarterly newletter *Scottish Bird News.*

Wildfowl Trust, Slimbridge, Gloucestershire GL2 7BT; Cambridge (Glos) 045-389 333.
Founded by Sir Peter Scott in 1946, the Wildfowl Trust concentrates on research into wildfowl and their conservation and has achieved remarkable success with breeding endangered species in captivity. It has several centres in England and Scotland with captive wildfowl and wild birds.

British Birds Rarities Committee, Hon Sec M.J. Rogers, Flat 4, Pentland Flats, St Mary's, Isles of Scilly TR21 0HM.

Binoculars and Telescopes
Some of the stockists listed below also offer repair services.
Bass & Bligh, 4 Briggate, Leeds.
Focalpoint, 14 Cogshall Lane, Comberbach, Northwich, Cheshire CW9 6BS.
Focus Optics, Church Lane, Corley, Coventry CV7 8BA.
Charles Frank Ltd, PO Box 5, Ronald Lane, Saxmundham, Suffolk IP17 2NL.
  Norwich Camera Centre, 20 White Lion Street, Norwich; 0603 21704.
  Kay Gee Cameras, 13 The Poultry, Nottingham NG1 2HW; 0602 506323.
  Edinburgh Cameras, 57 Lothian Road, Edinburgh; 031-229 3363.
A.R. Hawkins, 9 Marefair, Northampton.
Heron Optical Co, 23–25 Kings Road, Brentwood, Essex CM14 4ER; 0277 222230.
  3 Palace Street, Canterbury, Kent CT1 2DY; 0227 470023.
  Head Office and Mail Order, 3 Wates Way, Brentwood, Essex CM15 9TB; 0277 233122.
Herts Optical Services, 102a Victoria Street, St Albans, Herts.
In Focus, 204 High Street, Barnet, Herts.
Jessops of Leicester Ltd, Jessop House, 98 Scudamore Road, Leicester (mail order).
  Retail branches also in Aberdeen, Birmingham, Bournemouth, Brighton, Bristol, Cambridge, Croydon, Edinburgh, Glasgow, Hull, Leeds, Leicester,

Liverpool, London, Manchester, Newcastle, Norwich, Nottingham, Reading, Sheffield, Stoke, Wolverhampton.

Kay Optical Servicing, 89b London Road, Morden, Surrey.

Vic Odden's, 5 London Bridge Walk, London SE1.

Opticron, PO Box 81, 25 Lattimore Road, Unit 6, Marlborough Trading Estate, St Albans, Herts AL1 3NT.

Optima Leisure Products Ltd, Gilnow Mill Spa Road, Bolton, Lancs BL1 4LF.

Youngs, 40–42 Belvoir Street, Leicester.

Books
The Bird Bookshop, The Scottish Ornithologists' Club, 21 Regent Terrace, Edinburgh EH7 5BT.

Garden Bird Equipment
RSPB, The Lodge, Sandy, Bedfordshire SG19 2DL.

John E. Haith (Wild Bird Foods), Park Street, Cleethorpes, South Humberside DN35 7NF.

Jamie Wood Ltd, Cross Street, Polegate, Sussex.

Holidays and/or Birdwatching Courses
RSPB Development Department, The Lodge, Sandy, Bedfordshire SG19 2DL.

Aigas Field Centres, Beauly, Inverness-shire IV4 7AD.

Birdquest Ltd, 8 Albert Road East, Hale, Altrincham, Cheshire WA15 9AL.

Branta Travel Ltd, 20–24 Uxbridge Street, London W8 7TA.

Caledonian Wildlife, 30 Culduthel Road, Inverness IV2 4AP.

Cygnus Wildlife Holidays Ltd, 96 Fore Street, Kingsbridge, Devon TQ7 1PY.

Dutch Ornithological Tours, Purmer 70, 8244 AT Lelystad, The Netherlands.

Field Studies Council, Montford Bridge, Shrewsbury SY4 1HW.

Ornitholidays, 1/3 Victoria Drive, Bognor Regis, Sussex PO21 2PW.

Sahel Expeditions Ltd, Aucombe, Horningsham, Warminster BA12 7JN.

Sunbird, PO Box 76, Sandy, Bedfordshire SG19 1DF.

Magazines and Yearbook
Birds, sent to RSPB members – quarterly.

Bird Life, sent to YOC members – bi-monthly.

Bird Study, sent to BTO members – quarterly.

British Birds, Fountains, Park Lane, Blunham, Bedford MK44 3NJ – monthly.

Birdwatcher's Yearbook and Diary, edited by John E. Pemberton, Buckingham Press, 25 Manor Park, Maids Moreton, Buckingham MK18 1QX.

Portable Hides
Jamie Wood Ltd, Cross Street, Polegate, Sussex.